"A man who acquires the ability to take full possession of his

own mind may take possession of anything else to which he

is justly entitled."

Andrew Carnegie

Cover by SelfPubCovers.com/ACBookCovers/Joseph T.Riach

SUCCESSFUL LIVING BY JOSEPH TOM RIACH

The Secret World Of Self-Employment

Mastering The Art Of Making Money

Self-Improvement Should Be Fun!

Winning Big In Life And Business

The Simplest Sales Strategy

NOVELS BY JOSEPH T.RIACH

Too Early For A Glass Of Wine?

and

* New Mystery Thriller – Coming Soon! *

All available in Paperback and Ebook formats at Amazon (.com and .co.uk), Barnes and Noble and other leading book stores.

Contact Tom at www.tomriach.com

THE SECRET WORLD OF SELF-EMPLOYMENT

Joseph T.Riach

ISBN : 979-8722213129

CONTENTS

Introduction

Freedom!
Striking Out On Your Own

Action!
Small Steps For Giant Gains

Reward!
How To Be A Self-Employed Super Star

Conclusion

Joseph T.Riach

INTRODUCTION

ABOUT THE AUTHOR

Joseph Tom Riach lives and writes in the sunny south of Portugal. It is a far cry from his birth and upbringing in the rather chillier climes of 'the granite city' of Aberdeeen in north-east Scotland. He was educated at the town's famous Grammar School, as was Lord Byron in an earlier era.

In his early twenties Tom's independent spirit and drive saw him quickly become self-employed. He set up, acquired and operated a string of small businesses; then helped others to do likewise. He excelled as a 'hands-on' consultant to the self-employed and to owners of family enterprises; then to major companies and organisations too.

It is his experience and success in these endeavours which he writes about in his acclaimed 'Successful Living' and 'Personal Achievement' series of books. In these he presents a rich blend of his professional insights, personal views and fun stories, all of which reflect his dynamic and highly original approach to the world of business.

And his passion for writing extends to writing novels. His complete works are listed in the covers of this book.

Tom also hosts personal and business guidance courses for guests in the calm and tranquility of his Portuguese home. A home which three imperious cats generously permit Tom and wife Erna to share with them. All are happy.

Joseph T.Riach

ABOUT THIS BOOK

Readers of my books know that I am a fervent fan of self-employment. My enthusiasm for the sector is hardly surprising. I have been my own boss for almost my entire working life. Only for a short spell in my early days of earning was I in paid employments. Those experiences soon convinced both the employers involved and myself that my temperament was not best suited to the role of employee!

I am also a firm believer in an individual's right to the freedoms of thought, speech and action. As an employee, you are not always permitted to exercise these rights. What you must do in the work environment, your actions, will mostly be defined by your employer. You need to watch what you say and to whom. Even thoughts and beliefs can get you into hot water nowadays. A sad state of affairs not at all acceptable to any free spirit.

The alternative therefore is to work for yourself – think freely, speak candidly and act in your own best interests. That is what '*The Secret World Of Self-Employment*' is all about.

The book though is more than just another guide to the principles and practices of self-employment. It is quite different. Exceptional in fact. Why?

There are two reasons –

* Successful enterprises are born in the imagination. It is there that ideas are conceived, then nurtured. They are brought into reality by action. Then everyone can see the

business in operation and know what's going on. But they don't necessarily see all that's going on. Because much of what originates in the mind of an entrepreneur, stays in the mind of an entrepreneur. Their inner self houses their personal armoury of knowledge, ideas, strategies, tactics and tricks which they never share. It is in the minds of entrepreneurs that the secret world of self-employment exists.

* As an entrepreneur, I do not deal in theory. I am the original 'been there, seen it, done it' guy! I've been involved in a host of trade sectors, an encyclopedia of different enterprises and just about every self-employed situation imaginable - plus a good few more besides. I haven't just experienced the 'tricks of the trade', I originated many of them. It is these experiences which make up my secret world of self-employment.

Now, for the first time, I reveal these secrets of my self-employment. Ideas, tricks and actions which have remained concealed in my mind until now. Ways of working which will enable you to not just prosper on your own, but to take your enterprise into a different dimension altogether. Into a secret world of phenomenal achievement!

~

All books in my 'Successful Living and Personal Achievement' series contain passages extolling the virtues of self-employment and showing how to do it well. I believe it to be the essential element in a happy, free and prosperous life. This book though is my first manuscript dedicated exclusively to self-employment. As such, I've included some of those previous texts within the bulk of new material which make up the work. More so than just being a book about self-employment, this volume is unique in that it gives vivid insight to a hitherto unseen entrepreneurial world of the mind. The secret world of self-employment.

~

In keeping with all of my work, 'The Secret World Of Self-Employment' is written in simple language and an entertaining style. There is no jargon, fancy psychology or technical language to contend with. My view of life, and success in business, is underpinned by my sense of fun and simplicity. Those last attributes reside in the secret world of my mind and they are what you will find reflected in the ensuing pages. Enjoy the read.

Joseph Tom Riach, Author

Joseph T.Riach

BOOK 1

FREEDOM!

Striking Out On Your Own

Joseph T.Riach

Chapter 1

THE MINDSET OF AN ENTREPRENEUR

When I decided to become self-employed and set up my own business, I did not ask anyone's permission to do so. Why would I? Any such need would defeat the whole point of doing things for myself. Anyway, who would I ask? Family, friends? They'd only say, "Don't do it!". Or government? Heck no. They'd tie me down with endless red tape and regulations. No, I just went 'out there' and got on with it. I neither asked for nor expected assistance. I knew that I had to accept responsibility for my own actions, my success or my failure. Such self belief lies at the heart of any person intent on self-employment.

Part of that belief is that those not involved in the enterprise should mind their own affairs. Well-intentioned outsiders are the opposite of helpful. Governments should leave people and their businesses alone - unless they are doing direct harm to others. I believe in personal and business freedom, freedom of speech and freedom of action. I believe in a free market economy. All of these of course add up to accepting and enacting responsibility for my own thoughts and actions - nothing comes free in that respect.

My home town of Aberdeen in Scotland was at one time Europe's largest fishing port. Thousands of people were employed in the fish industry which comprised everything from trawlermen to dock workers to fish houses, fish processing factories, cold storage and transportation. As a young kid growing up, many of my first after-school and weekend jobs were 'in the fish'.

Quite suddenly the industry died. The fishing boats left ... and the oil supply vessels moved in. Yes, oil had been discovered in the North Sea. Aberdeen would enjoy a second bonanza as the oil capital of Europe! The economy thrived and entrepreneurs formerly benefiting from opportunities created in fishing turned their attention to the big bucks to be made in North Sea support and ancillary services. I was one of them.

My activities were actually two or three times down the line from direct oil related businesses but I was in little doubt that it was the front line exploration and pumping of oil and gas that was the prime creator of the wealth which I, and so many others, were enjoying.

In due course my business activities took me to further flung corners of Britain, and Europe too. Many of these places had none of the wealth and attendant infrastructure which first fishing and then oil had created in the north-east of Scotland. Yet I still found opportunities to create businesses. Lots of them. So many in fact that it led me to a startling conclusion.

What I realised was this – *You don't need a 'Klondike situation' in order to prosper as an entrepreneur!*

Although such a thriving scenario encourages speculation, business creation and commercial activity, that in itself is not the main driver in people's entrepreneurial motivation. The primary driver behind any entrepreneur is the ambition to be their own man or woman, control their own destiny and be the best they possibly can be. With that mindset you'll find opportunities and succeed anywhere!

Entrepreneurs invent solutions, create enterprises and make fortunes everywhere. They thrive in even the most improbable places. Be it deserts, jungles, mountain tops or frozen wastes, you'll find someone profiting from an opportunity they've identified. And they'll have identified that niche from first having an enquiring and inventive mind.

The entrepreneurial mindset is unique in that it must be creative, communicative and highly motivated to succeed, yet open to risk and failure. The key to entrepreneurial success therefore is little to do with the location of the business or the business sector. It is everything to do with the determination and the characteristics of the individual.

Before embarking on your self-employed adventure and becoming your own boss, ask yourself - Do you possess the appropriate mindset? – the mindset of an entrepreneur!

Joseph T.Riach

Chapter 2

FIRING THE BOSS

What many people don't understand is that wealth won't bring them happiness in life. It actually works the other way around. Find happiness first then wealth will follow.

Most people want to be happy but they often don't know what they are looking for. Inevitably they never find it. Even if they did find it, since they don't know what they are looking for, how would they ever recognise it?

There are those who associate happiness only with financial wealth. Their view is mistaken. Most such people truly want to be rich. Yet even those, if asked to define the exact amount of money and assets they wish to acquire and the time frame within which they intend to acquire it, will be incapable of answering. How can you get to where you hope to be when you don't know where you are going?

This is not to say that happiness and material wealth cannot coexist in your life but you first must understand that true wealth, and therefore happiness, is an attitude of the mind. Purely pursuing money can become an obsession which prevents you from enjoying life. Conversely, living in poverty is no walk in the park either! The fact is that money is an excellent servant but a tyrannical master. What you need is a balanced and a planned approach to achieving first, wealth in its broadest sense through happiness and second, happiness through your wealth. How to do it? There's a simple solution

The key to happiness is within everyone. With the key you will know without doubt if you are happy and if you are doing what it takes to make you happy. Here it is -

Are you doing what you love doing?

If so, then you will by definition be adding value to other people too. Doing what you truly enjoy always rubs off on others. If you are not doing what you love to do, then you are not happy. Do you spend your time dreaming about what you would like to be doing? Because, if you never actually do what you dream about, you are inevitably unhappy. When you never do what you really enjoy, you have given up on your dreams. Staying in work and life situations which you loathe, weighs you down, saps your spirit and does not lead to wealth, spiritual or material.

So be brave and act. Do it now. Do not permit your fears to over-ride your dreams of discovering those things which you really enjoy. Know what you are looking for and where you are going. Find the things you love. That is the key to happiness. Wealth, in all its forms, will follow.

In order to be the master of your own destiny you must become your own boss and work for yourself. There is no other way.

Sure there are those who work for corporations, companies and employers who enjoy varying degrees of autonomy but few, if any, of these people decide exactly what work they will do, when and where they will do it and how much they will be remunerated for their efforts. And these four factors –

* Choice

* Time

* Location

and

* Reward

– are what determine whether it is you or someone else who owns your life and pretty much everything in it. Look at it this way, let's consider life generally.

Would you accept a life in which you had no say over what you could or could not do each day? Would you be happy to be instructed as to what your actions should or should not be? Do you understand that time, as in real life time, is your most precious asset? Why would you give your most precious asset away to a third party or tolerate being told when and how you must use it? Why would you exchange it for a paltry financial return fixed by another party and never remotely close to its real value? (Time is in fact invaluable).

Why would you accept rewards, usually just material and therefore largely worthless, which fall far below your own valuation of your own self worth and your expectation of what you deserve from life?

The answers of most people to all of these questions would quite rightly be that they would not even consider, let alone agree to those terms. They are totally unacceptable. If you would not accept those criteria in your life generally then why accept them in your place of work?

Once you have that incredibly simple point firmly fixed in your mind, you can understand that it is only by rejecting the limitations of subservient employment in your working life that you can ensure that you enjoy the freedom of choice, use of your own time and reward for your efforts that you demand from life generally.

Only as your own boss setting the working conditions that suit you and meet your own requirements as regards choice, self-determination and the rewards of quality life as well as material gain, can you be sure to experience in life generally all the happiness and joy which is your birthright. Only when fully in control of your choices, your time and your rewards can you truly control your life and all that results in it.

So, determine to experience in life all the exhilaration and joy which is your birthright. Exercise your freedom of choice to think, say and do the things you want to do, where and when you want and in the manner that you want. Don't be deflected from your course. Dare to choose self-employment.

~

Before setting up in business on my own account at the tender age of just twenty-three years I had already had at least that same number of jobs! Another staggering statistic is that I had been fired from more than half of them!

Did I have so many jobs and get sacked with such regularity because I did not work hard enough? Not so. I was generally regarded as a harder grafter than most. I actually incurred the wrath of some longer established workers for doing too much and thus increasing pressure on them to equal my effort!

Was I fired for not being smart enough? Nope, not that either. In fact I was considered to be something of a bright spark. Within a short time of arriving in an employ my imaginative ideas and opinions became valued. They were sought after by management and work mates alike.

So why did I keep getting fired?

Simple ... I was overly confident, cocky, carefree and cantankerous. I was loud-mouthed and aggressive. I was strong-willed, spoke my mind and believed that I knew everything – aahh the arrogance of youth!

I was particularly dismissive of many of my bosses. Some I considered to be mediocre at best. In later life (not much later) I established that I had in many instances been close to the mark on that score. Much of company management was, and still is, unimaginative and lacking in creativity and entrepreneurial flair.

In several instances I was paid off because my superiors were wary of my ability. I can size up situations quickly and conceive solutions which others can't see. That scared them. Rather than embracing my talent and 'bringing me onside', as an astute boss would do, they were terrified of having their limitations exposed. Others simply 'borrowed' my ideas, claimed the credit for themselves and then fired me. I even fell victim to the classic 'set up' of stolen goods being placed in my pockets to be 'discovered' later by the very management stooge who had put them there!

But I'm grateful for all of that because I learned, and I learned quickly.

So, am I the kind of guy you would consider qualified to teach you, with exact step by step instructions, how to get seriously wealthy and quickly? Let's find out, here are the instructions :

Step 1 : *The most important one - Go right now to your boss, barge unannounced into his office and verbally abuse him. I guarantee that you will feel like a million dollars! .... now that's serious wealth!*

Step 2 : Your boss will either :

(a) The smart move – Immediately promote you to MD of the company and award you a massive pay increase for being the guy with the biggest walnuts in town

or

(b) The most likely move – Fire you on the spot

In the event that your boss follows Step 2 (b) then move on to Step 3

Step 3 : *Set up your own business and go to work for yourself!*

Yes it's that simple. And be sure to choose a business where you're doing something that you really enjoy, something for which you have a real passion, rather than just any old business or the one which you think that you can make most money from. Take it from me, if you do something you love (and preferably which helps other people too) then you will feel free and seriously happy. That's far and away the most important thing. Then all the other stuff, wealth and trappings, will follow .... if you want them!

That's it.

Now here's a question for you :

Do you believe that the information which I have just given to you is a

- **Credible**

- Serious
- Valuable
- Disclosure - capable of making you seriously wealthy were you to employ it?

Or do you think that I'm just that twenty-three year old rookie 'avin a larff?

There's no right or wrong answer to that. But I do assure you that, dependent on the conclusion you arrive at, rests your chances of ever getting to be seriously wealthy!

Joseph T.Riach

Chapter 3

WHO TO TRUST?

Part of the skill of owning your own future and being self-employed is knowing who to listen to and when, and who to ignore. The simple truth is that a heck of a lot of opinion that will come your way is simply not worth hearing. You'll receive 'advice' from anybody and everybody. The whole world and his dog will overnight become experts on your case – people who don't really know you, people who don't know what they're talking about and people who are really giving themselves advice rather than addressing you or your situation.

Very occasionally there may be thoughtful observations or helpful comments emanate from such sources but so many of them are so wrong so much of the time as to be worthless, even damaging. I suggest that you ignore them all. Most of such advice I received in my formative years and early times in business amounted to - "Give up!" I formed the habit of ignoring all that and going my own way. Things worked out just fine.

So who do you ask or seek guidance from regarding your proposed new way forward? Are there specialists in the field of owning your own future to whom you can turn? Not many. There are a number of reasons for that.

The first and simplest reason is that only you can be you! No-one else can say, "If I were you I'd ..." - because they are not you! When someone is not the person actually involved in the decision they are not subject to the same personality, preferences, thought processes, pressures, emotions and past experiences as the perpetrator. Also, because they are not you and are looking in from the outside, their advice is almost certain to be prejudiced towards caution. Which brings me to the second reason regarding advice.

People – friends, relatives, colleagues – don't want to be responsible for your failure. So they are not going to give you cavalier encouragement. More so, there will be many who want you to fail. Sad but true, but those who are unwilling to make any effort to improve themselves or their situation take pleasure in denouncing the enterprise of others and in seeing them fail. It's best to stay away from such people.

POWER POINT - *"Ignore others' worthless comments and go your own way."*

Also steer clear of accountants or lawyers. These are the professionals who the majority of people will seek advice from regarding a new enterprise. They are, in reality, not well placed to help as regards the entrepreneurial aspect of your decision. In other words, as with family who might not want to give guidance which they feel might lead to failure, so too is the case with these professionals. They can only, and will only, ever advise caution for fear of their professional reputation. Their opinions as to entrepreneurism are worthless. They are a long way from being experts in that respect.

Anyway, and lastly, never trust so-called experts. Don't even trust the word 'expert'. Especially when it is used by someone about themselves! I loathe the word and refuse to use it – ever.

POWER POINT - *"Never trust an 'expert'!"*

I do acknowledge the term specialist. If you are looking for guidance in any area of life or business, seek out a specialist in the particular area or discipline in which you want help. A consultant well versed and better, well practiced, in their area of speciality But a word of warning here too.

There exists what I call 'blue chip consultants'; those who have progressed from school to university, studied for a degree and then gone into practice as a 'consultant'. Everything they know they have learned from a book. Nothing wrong with that as far as it goes except that they will never actually have done the thing that they are advising you about! Plus, they'll only ever advise, never get involved.

Then there are those like me, what I call a 'hands on consultant'. There is nothing that I will give guidance about that I have not actually done myself, bumps, bruises and all. I know what I'm talking about from real practical experience. Everything that I write about in this book for example, and all my other writings, are true accounts of real events and my experiences pertaining to them.

Above all, I am an entrepreneur. I am inclined to give adventurous advice and encouragement. There is little wrong with that. After all, it is only by being adventurous that you can possibly gain. Misplaced caution means by definition standing still, going nowhere, achieving nothing. Guidance in that direction is totally worthless.

POWER POINT - *"Only by being adventurous can you possibly gain."*

However (yes there's a however) not everyone is equipped to go forward in this way. Some people, however well-intentioned just do not possess the qualities, or lack the dedication, required to succeed in working on their own account. You must be sure that you are suited to meet the challenges ahead.

If you were an employer with a job vacancy you would interview candidates for the position and as an applicant for a vacancy you'd expect to be interviewed. You would actually be rather unimpressed by a boss who gave you the job just because you turned up. In that case you wouldn't have been evaluated for the work and could feel neither valued nor sure of your ability to successfully fill the position.

So, before embarking on your self-employed adventure, set up an interview for the post. Only on this occasion it will be an interview – with yourself!

Chapter 4

DO YOU KNOW WHO YOU ARE?

Do you know who you are? Have you ever thought to interview yourself in order to find out how you really measure up to the task of working for yourself? To find out if you really are the right candidate for the job? It's not such a crazy idea.

Should you fail the interview then you can save yourself the time, cost and trouble of setting up in business. Or at least learn that you must first go to school on yourself in order to better prepare for self-employment. If you pass the interview then you can march forward confident that you have a basic grasp of what's required.

Here's how to go about preparing and assessing yourself for suitability to be employed - by yourself for yourself!

You should understand that successful entrepreneurs possess certain common characteristics. Looking at what these traits are and adopting them will help to prepare you for both the interview and the challenges beyond. What is it that your new boss is looking for in you?

First know that – **Entrepreneurs Are Leaders.**

You may only be leading yourself (especially in the early days) but you still must understand and be able to employ leadership skills. You, the employee, needs to have sound leadership from you, the boss!

You must also possess - **Passion and Self-Belief.**

Passion is about both loving what you do and feeling so strongly about it that there is nothing else you would choose to do or be happier doing. You will believe absolutely that you deserve to do the thing in life which you most enjoy; and that you possess the strength and resolve to accomplish all that you set out to do. Nothing and no-one will stop you from taking the necessary steps to achieve your goal.

The next requirement is that you are a – **Bold Risk Taker**.

Most entrepreneurs are natural risk takers and bold with it. It takes more than a great idea to start up in business. You must have the resolve to stand by your idea and keep pushing forward. Especially in those times (and there'll be plenty of them) when it seems as if you are wasting your time. You also need the courage to know when things cannot improve and it's time to change course.

You also have to be bold in getting in front of your audience and telling them who you are and what you are doing. The majority of people cannot do that. If 'shouting about your business' embarrasses you in some way then self-employment is not for you.

You have to be bold in asking for what you want. To most people it's totally terrifying to ask someone, often a complete stranger, for something that you really want. Your fear is misplaced. When you ask directly and spell out exactly what you want, you will be amazed by how positively people respond.

POWER POINT - *"Ask directly and spell out exactly what it is that you want from people and situations."*

Take the risk and ask for what you want. The worst case scenario is that they say, "No," - hardly life threatening. In that case rephrase your question or ask, "Why?" or simply move on to the next situation.

Risk taking is a part of business. To the outsider, a risk taker often appears to be 'skating on thin ice' and yes, certain situations can be financially and emotionally uncomfortable. But it's the capacity to make bold choices and take necessary actions which singles you out as a true entrepreneur. Besides which, as I write elsewhere, there are ways of mitigating risk so that what appears risky to others is actually anything but.

You'll also need to be – **Flexible And Resilient.**

When I first met one of my millionaire mentors in my early days in business, he seemed to me to be constantly changing his mind. So much so that I wondered how he could possibly have become so successful with such an approach. I challenged him about it. His response was that he'd become successful precisely because he did alter his thinking constantly. He was, you see, constantly analysing and reviewing things. This in order to ensure that he'd missed nothing and arrived at the optimum conclusion. In due course I followed his example (boy I'm glad I did) and I suggest that you do too.

Of course you must be focussed and unshakeable on your big goals but, in tandem with that, you should be flexible with things day to day. When overly rigid in your approach you can miss important details, aspects and nuances of significance; also opportunities, both major and minor, some of which could help you achieve your bigger goal more easily, at less cost or more speedily.

As regards speed, yes of course you must be able to think on your feet, make quick decisions. There isn't always time to dally. Opportunities can be lost by hanging about. To be a great entrepreneur you'll often have to move fast.

You need to be resilient too. Being your own boss can be really hard. You're on your own and, more often than not, out on a limb. Don't expect others to be with you or supportive. They'll mostly think that you're wasting your time. Resilience is what keeps you going, both when you get hit with a big failure (yes that will happen) or just the everyday knocks and bruises. It's essential that you're a bouncy person – when you get knocked over you just bounce back up!

The last quality you'll need to look for in yourself is – **A Self-Effacing Sense Of Humour.**

Yes, you'd better be able to laugh at yourself! Get in first with the funny side of things because, if you don't, others sure will. That's no bad thing. You need to see your endeavours as from a bird's eye view. That means being dispassionate.

From that vantage point you'll see what you are doing right, what you are doing not so well and the things that are just plain hideous! You will see what is working well and also where you are drifting off course. Relax, re-evaluate, smile, shrug and get back to work

Remember – *The more you have fun, the more you'll get done!*

The Interview

Okay, those are the qualities you are looking for in yourself as your own boss. Now on to the actual interview.

If you've been with a company as a manager you'll already

know that identifying the stars of the future is not easy. You will almost certainly have experienced the stress of recruiting an employee who seems to excel on paper but fails to live up to their hype in practice.

As the manager of your own business recruiting yourself to work for you, how do you ensure that you are picking the best person for the role, a candidate with the skills, know-how, experience and extra 'something' that makes you stand out? What key questions are you going to ask yourself?

You'll need a planned approach to identify the qualities that will make you exceptional in the role. It's only by getting up close and personal with yourself and engaging yourself face to face, that you can get an honest sense of your abilities. After all, you'll be selling yourself to yourself during interview, so you'll be able to assess just how you approach self-employment generally, clients and suppliers first hand.

Make the most of the interview. Don't freestyle or ask the same tired questions. Build a framework of key competencies that you know your next incarnation as a self-employed star needs to possess.

Here are the questions :

Are You A Potential Sales Star?

The reason I start with the above question is simple. You might have the finest goods or service on offer but unless you can sell them then you'll go nowhere – fast! I've often written of how my own self-employment rocketed only after I shifted my emphasis on to the selling side of the business. Whatever other business disciplines you may excel in, you will only reach your full potential when you master selling.

No other part of your enterprise is as critical to success as your ability to market and sell your offer. You might wish to read my book on the subject – *The Simplest Sales Strategy.*

Are you a self-starter and able to manage yourself?

Ask yourself how your last few weeks in employment looked and request a detailed description of your activities from start to finish. From this you'll get a sense of your drive, enthusiasm and ability to organise, stay motivated and put in simple hard work. If you are uncertain about what you've been doing, alarm bells may ring. Everyone can have forgetful moments, but as a good entrepreneur/self-employed person you will have come to interview armed with your diary to refresh your memory about past achievements, contracts won, successful outcomes, people and places and promotional meetings you intend to undertake.

How do you invest in your career?

Ask yourself what your favourite business strategies and business books, gurus and learning resources are. Seek evidence that you are responsible for your own development and learning, whether getting professional development in your current role, reading the latest blogs and periodicals, or attending networking and other industry events to brush up on your skills. Look for evidence of associated interests which reveal a well rounded intellect capable of discussing life and business in general and able to have informed conversations with colleagues, suppliers and customers while displaying your in-depth, specialist knowledge.

How are your presentation, negotiation and deal-closing skills?

Find out how you organise presentations, what you enjoy about doing them and how effective you believe you are. This is an ideal task to set yourself within interview to test your skills in action. Similarly, you can set yourself practical exercises with friends to test your skills at negotiation and deal closing

Are you flexible? Are you creative?

Think back to past instances in your employment where things have gone wrong and you were forced to think on your feet. Were you quick thinking? Was your attitude proactive and customer focussed? Be honest with yourself, everyone makes mistakes, the key issue is how you responded to them.

Are you tenacious and able to bounce back from rejection?

Look at what have been your biggest challenges and how you responded to them. Consider your own body language, get in front of a mirror and mimic the ways you think you move, facial expressions and gestures. Also the way that you talk, how you sound, in various situations. Do you express with these your true feelings – anger, hurt, rejection – or can you contain yourself with prepared responses to suit any circumstance. Have you always been prepared, poised and persuasive?

How much knowledge do you have about the techniques of your trade?

Do you know what your top open-ended questions for initial contact are and how familiar with and practiced are you in the key skills of communication, negotiating and closing?

Can you be more than just a one trick pony?

As a self-employed business proprietor do you possess a wide appreciation of your functions and roles within your own organisation and understand that you will have many duties to perform? What else will you be doing to drive your company's success - 'everything' is not good enough, be specific. Look for signs within yourself of someone engaged in more than just making money.

Are you a leader?

Does that sound like a particularly fatuous question given that there's just yourself in the business? Well it's not, far from it. Being your own boss and having the duty of instilling motivation and discipline on yourself is harder by far than managing other people. Fail on this and your business fails. Be ruthlessly honest in addressing this question. Look within yourself as a candidate able to lead yourself and with the potential to develop, coach and mentor younger and less-experienced employees as your business grows.

Are You Passionate And Engaging?

Do you have development potential? Can you progress within all your functions and grow the business. Are you authentic, honest with yourself and others? There is nothing worse than reeling off prepared answers to yourself, the only person you're kidding is yourself. Do you engage others with your eyes, your words and your body language? Do you create emotion and response in yourself as the interviewer with your answers and interactions as the candidate. If you are authentic and have a real passion for your proposed venture then, as an entrepreneur, that carries more weight than formal training and a lack of experience.

This is because it is better for you to have the right potential to put yourself through your own training courses and structure, rather than a you who is not sufficiently motivated and simply goes through the motions for the you that's paying your wages. You need to be something more; a team player who will commit to your organisation and be excited and ready to help build its success.

Can You Laugh At Yourself – Really?

You have more than likely heard the maxim, "Take your work seriously but never yourself." Do you really practice that? You should. Nobody likes a self-important sod and, if they don't like you, they are less likely to trust you. If they don't trust you they won't do business with you. Lighten up. But be a serious, dedicated professional too.

Having a sense of perspective is absolutely critical. Don't get too wrapped up in what you're doing. Be able to step back and see the humour in situations. Laugh a lot. Clients, employees, suppliers – all will love you for it. *The more you have fun, the more you'll get done!*

Interview Completed

Now, having completed the interview and candidate review process, are you prepared to offer yourself the position of being self-employed by yourself?

If yes … then congratulations! You dare to be different and take ownership of your own future. Time to become your own boss.

Joseph T.Riach

Chapter 5

YOU GOT THE JOB!

So you've passed the interview and selected yourself to employ yourself as a self-employed person! But doing what?

The obvious answer to that is that you will choose a business involved in a trade or profession of which you are knowledgeable. Also one where you expect to make good money. More important than either of those factors, and a consideration which is surprisingly overlooked by a vast number of fledgling entrepreneurs, is that you should choose to do something which you really enjoy. A pursuit for which you have a real passion. When you fail to make that your number one consideration you will be setting yourself on a course which at best will lead to you becoming a slave to your business and at worst will lead to misery and ruin. So choose to do something which you love!

POWER POINT - *"Choose only work which you truly enjoy and which helps other people."*

In tandem with that, choose an activity which will help other people. Surprised? You shouldn't be. You'll derive great pleasure from helping others and this will reflect on the happiness at your work factor achieved by being involved on a daily basis with an activity which you thoroughly enjoy performing. Doing what you love plus helping others in the process is the sure fire way to a happy life (your primary goal) and from there to making profit and being materially wealthy – if that's what you want.

"If that's what I want? Of course I want a profitable business!" I hear your incredulous cries. But take it from me, the surest way to achieve that is by pursuing, not money or material gain, but a happy life appreciative of life's simple pleasures and helping others. So, find a niche that satisfies those aims. What is a niche?

A niche market is the subset of the market on which a specific product or service is focussed. The market niche defines the product features aimed at satisfying specific market needs, as well as the price range, production quality and the demographics that it is intended to impact. It is also a small market segment. Every product and service can be defined by its market niche.

I, for example, in my work as a business consultant, targeted small companies and the self-employed. That niche is where I enjoyed working and where I believed I could help people. I tailored the services I offered to suit the needs of clients in that sector. The work was (still is) my passion.

To me, niche and passion are two words which fit together like peas in a pod. You can't have one without the other. Spending your time working in a sector, or doing something that you're not absolutely enthusiastic about, is an utter waste of precious life time.

POWER POINT - *"Let your passion determine your niche and then both will define your success."*

One of my first passions and my first experience of bringing the house down, in the theatrical sense, was when, as a four year old, I sang 'I am a little teapot' at a holiday camp talent show. I won first prize. It was both the beginning and the end of my stage career as a public entertainer. A case of coming in with a bang and going out at the top!

The next time I brought the house down, this time almost literally, was many years later when I decided to personally remove a partition wall in my Georgian era townhouse. I proudly showed my work in progress to a structural engineer friend who, far from being impressed, was mortified by what he saw. He immediately closed down my work and the entire building. It was on the point of collapse.

Two years, a multitude of architects, lawyers and builders, tons of steel girders from the foundations to the top (fourth) floor and a bank account hovering between life and death in intensive care, later, I moved back into the property, now fully reinforced and magnificently restored. My sanity is yet to experience such a rebirth. Forget nightmare. This episode in my life equated to a full blooded horror movie with several sequels and a monster that refused to die.

The result of the experience is that today I will not even hammer a nail into a wall. It's not that the nail might bend or that I'll suffer a bloodied thumb, it's the terror that the whole wall will cave in! I leave that work to people who both specialise in that kind of thing and enjoy doing it.

In my school days I excelled in English literature, languages, geography, history and maths. I whizzed through my exams in these subjects without even opening a book. They were easy to me. I enjoyed them. There were also mandatory classes each week in art, woodwork and metalwork. I gained useful knowledge about these practical disciplines but was never fired up by them. I didn't have the enthusiasm to see myself as a Picasso, Moore or Rodin. Therefore those subjects were never going to be my forte. But I did try them.

POWER POINT - *"Try this and that; find your passion; establish your niche."*

And that's what you as an entrepreneur or self-employed business person must do. Tinker around with a number of business possibilities. Try this and that. Find out what works for you and what doesn't. Experience failure, learn from it. You'll come out the other end of the process with broad general knowledge and ability which will stand you in good stead. You'll thus be prepared to avoid the bent nail and bloodied thumb disasters and specialise in the area which gives you most pleasure and satisfaction. That's where to establish your business niche.

If you enjoy restoring old buildings (and earning a fortune at my expense) become an architect, engineer, builder or tradesman. If you enjoy bringing the house down (literally) become a demolition contractor. If you enjoy performing on stage then become a singing teapot.

And, if all else fails ... become like me!

But where to begin ..... ?

When you first strike out on your own and become your own boss you will, in all likelihood, already know a bit about bosses from previous work as an employee. Even though you are starting off with no employees under you, you still need to manage yourself. What you've learned from your ex-bosses is going to come in handy either way.

From a self-employed perspective it really doesn't matter if your former bosses were good, bad or indifferent in your eyes. You had to live with them and should have learned from them all. You'll have found it more difficult to do a good job under a bad boss of course and yet such a boss should have taught you a lot.

I see the bad boss experience kind of like an athlete training on sand dunes or on the beach, as I do. It's damned hard work but it toughens you up for the real event. When you transfer on to a dedicated running surface you can go like the wind. In life all pursuits should be like that - the hard work in the preparation, the performance itself pure fun.

POWER POINT - "*The hard work in life or business is in the preparation.*"

One benefit of being under the control of a bad boss is that it can incentivise you to strike out on your own; the 'I must get out of here' syndrome. Working with a good boss can also encourage you to go it alone, but in a quite different way. He will have created a happy and productive working environment, thus demonstrating what is achievable.

You will never see eye to eye all the time with any boss, good or bad, but, whereas the bad boss will simply beat you down a good boss will most likely welcome your views and input. Your ideas may be at odds with his but disagreeing with a good boss is a quite different story from working under a bad one!

We all need to be able to take direction, even from ourselves(!), so listen, be flexible and take criticism on board. Such is life. As your own boss you are duty bound to work things out for yourself and take responsibility for all your thoughts and actions. Be open to what the boss says – whether that means you, your boss, your client or your partner in life!

With any boss you should start from the position of trusting that the boss knows what he's doing. So, in your self-employed role have total belief in yourself. It may not always be clear to others why you are doing things in a particular way, but that's because they cannot see the bigger picture. Outsiders can only see things from a limited or ignorant point of view. You as an entrepreneur (or any boss in any business) may be looking for something others have not thought of; you may be intent on actions that would never occur to anyone else.

Either way, all bosses want what is best for the bigger picture, as opposed to the limited view from one employee's or one outsider's perspective, because they see their affairs globally as if looking at a map from above. No, they're not always God (only sometimes) but they generally know best how to achieve things. As your own boss, shut out external interference and trust your instinct and judgement to know what's right too. Then most often you will be!

POWER POINT - *"Trust your gut instinct. It will serve you well."*

As your own boss you will need to exercise tremendous self-discipline. I consider all discipline and particularly self-discipline to be an essential element in any person's success strategy. Without it you will almost certainly fail. Writing, as I am doing here, is a good example of an activity in which it would be impossible to flourish without strong self-discipline. The only person making me do it is ... myself!

POWER POINT - *"Successful achievers possess and exercise relentless self-discipline."*

As your own boss you are the only one who can ensure that you turn up for work. You will have to learn not to continually put things off 'til tomorrow! Procrastination can be one of your greatest enemies. Without an external boss to enforce time management it's just so easy for you to delay getting down to work and to find excuses for not acting now. But there's always work to be done – if not in one area of your business then in another.

Just like reporting for a 'proper' job, establish your hours of work and stick to them. Eight in the morning until mid-day, two-thirty to five-thirty in the afternoon works for many. Or work flexi hours, whatever suits you and the kind of work that you are involved in. But find the sort of schedule which works best for you .... and then stick to it.

Whatever agenda you choose for yourself exercise strict discipline. If you don't, you'll achieve nothing. When you do impose discipline you'll be surprised at how much you can get done and the quality of work that you produce.

Your discipline must be relentless. It's not a one day or one week thing. It's 'forever'.

Joseph T.Riach

Chapter 6

GET SET, GO!

A good starting point in self-employment, and one which many newly self-employed people pursue, is to work as a commission sales person or affiliate marketer. In these cases you will have no goods or services of your own to produce but rather you sell the goods or services of another company, preferably a well established one. In this way you avoid all the hassle of devising a service or of manufacturing goods with the attendant work and cost of their creation, physical storage and movement. You simply sell the goods or service. Your host company arranges the delivery and you pick up a commission. But you are self-employed, and arrange your own hours of work and modus operandi.

Which company to represent? I presume that you want to be the best at what you do, so better promote the goods or services of a brand which trades in excellence, are quite simply superb at what they do and are the best of the best. Why settle for less?

I recommend that you do the following :

* Work, train and study to be the very best representative that you can possibly be

* Work only with those who you trust implicitly, can look up to and learn from

* Sell only the finest product or service, one in which you have total belief and confidence

* Represent only a company which provides the highest quality product or service

* Represent only a company which provides the highest quality training, support and back up

* Represent only a company which pays the highest commissions and does so timeously and without quibble

* Represent a company and work only with people of integrity

Finding a host company which satisfies just two or three of those criteria may well be difficult. More so to find one which satisfies them all. Don't be discouraged. Such entities do exist and, by definition, will consist of people who, from the top down, are endowed with the highest ethical and professional standards. The result being that they create a centre of excellence to which they can bring the brightest and best talent – hopefully you!

I repeat, if you intend to be the best (and why would you want to be anything less)? then you must work with the best. Time spent finding them will pay you handsomely.

POWER POINT - *"To be the best, work only with the best."*

When you do very well in your commission selling or affiliate marketing career you may well, in due course, earn enough to enable you to emerge from the protective shield of a host company and expand into other areas of business and self enterprise. You will have gained the experience, contacts, knowledge and financial muscle to be able to accomplish this with a confidence born from your success. It's a route to riches followed by many successful entrepreneurs.

I myself did very well indeed from working as a commission salesman although I didn't start out in that way. My first business was transport related, an activity of which I had scant knowledge at the time although I had worked for a few hauliers and delivery companies. But I learned quickly and moved into consultancy work on the back of my experience.

I laboriously built up my reputation as a trustworthy source of business advice for more than seven years before a business colleague persuaded me to integrate into my advisory work some commission selling for the company he represented. It was then that my business really took off!

Such was my success in that sphere that, in my freelance roll as a Senior Offshore Investment and Corporate Planning Consultant with major London merchant bank investment arm, Hill Samuel Financial Services, I qualified regularly as an international conference delegate and soon became their leading UK producer of new mortgage business. As a result of which my business consultancy (me) was employed by several major companies to enlighten their sales teams with regard to my success strategies. Thereby furthering even more my own success and my financial well-being.

All of which allowed me to establish, acquire and operate several more substantial businesses than those I had run previously. So I know that being a commission sales person or affiliate marketer is a good way to build up experience in self-employment as well as the overall profitability of your enterprise.

Still, there are pitfalls to avoid in order to prosper in this area. Avoid the following mistakes and you'll find success easier and quicker to come by :

Stand Out From The Crowd

As a sales agent (or in any self-employed capacity) you will most likely find that there are a host of others out there in the market place selling the same product or service as yourself. You will often find that your fellow agents are your main competitors. So you need to differentiate yourself from all the others in order to stand out from the crowd.

In my case, I did this in five ways :

1. I studied to become, and promoted myself as, a leading authority, the professional the others came to

2. I promoted myself and my business consultancy - my brand, not the products off which I earned commissions

3. I sought locations where there was no other presence and went there however remote and difficult to get to

4. I targeted potential buyers within the niche more specifically and more determinedly than the opposition

5. I looked at the traditional sales channels/methods for the products then did the exact opposite (contrarian, thinking outside the box).

POWER POINT - *"Compete by not competing but by thinking outside the box and finding innovative ways to get to clients first and make an exclusive offer."*

I also capitalised on the fact that many of the other agents, both those employed directly by the host companies and freelancers such as myself, lacked both product knowledge and sales ability. In other words, they did not work hard enough to be the best; at being up to date and au fait with everything going on in the industry and all that there was to know about their product and how to promote it most effectively. Don't let this be you!

As well as insuring that you are totally prepared to be the best, learn to not sell rather than to sell. Confused? You needn't be. You'll find all the answers in my *The Simplest Sales Strategy* book. The gist of the message though is that people try too hard to sell. Don't let this be you.

My Experience

At the beginning of my career I set out with the aim of creating material wealth and becoming successful. Although I worked tirelessly I achieved little of either. However, over time, through experience and with the counsel of those older and far wiser than myself, I learned that the sure route to real wealth, both material and spiritual, lay not in working on the commercial aspects of life or business but was to be found in concentrating all of my efforts in helping others.

That is what I did. I concentrated purely on helping others. It is from that strategy that every kind of wealth imaginable flowed. I can absolutely assure you that, whatever you want from life, the best way to get it is to focus your energy in helping others.

If you want higher self-esteem then find ways to boost someone else's self-esteem.

If you want to raise your positive spirit then assist someone else to raise theirs.

If you want more happiness in life the smartest way to get it is to help someone else achieve it.

When you give generously of your time and effort in these ways then in due course you will discover as if by magic that the biggest beneficiary of your efforts is .. you! You'll become spiritually rich, relaxed, confident and inwardly calm. One fully in harmony with your inner self. From there you'll attract every kind of wealth imaginable!

POWER POINT - *"Would you rather do business with someone pushy who you don't know or with someone trustworthy who you do know?"*

Rather than selling, instead work at getting to know your clients and establishing a relationship with them. The psychology is simple. Would you rather do business with someone pushy who you don't really know or with someone of integrity who you do know? Easy, isn't it? It's all about trust. Remember, your ideal business is one which you passionately enjoy doing and which helps other people. Help your target audience, don't sell them.

Don't however confuse helping people and being friendly with being a pushover. Weak-willed people do not succeed in business. More than that, it is assertive and persistent people who do succeed.

POWER POINT - *"The assertive and persistent succeed in business, the weak-willed fail."*

~

As a boy I was pathetically naive at times; far too trusting and overly eager to please. It was two older boys, capitalising on my gullibility, who first introduced me to the "You rob the bank and I'll run" philosophy.

Their dastardly plan was to saunter by the fruit shop and, if all was clear, signal to me to follow up and nick apples from the street display for all three of us. They wandered up the road, gave their all-clear signal, I followed on and grabbed the apples and ... was immediately collared from behind by the massive fist of an angry shop owner!

My 'friends' scuttled off laughing hilariously at the success of their set up while I was hauled inside and subjected to a terrible grilling with threats of police and parental involvement. But I sobbed the apologies of a terrified eight year old and was eventually released without further action. I won't claim that I never again nicked an apple but I did learn not to assume the risk in a situation while affording someone else the potential benefit.

POWER POINT - *"Do not assume risk or liability on someone else's behalf."*

Several years later I was approached to sign for a football club of which the president was the self-same fruit merchant! When we met and I reminded him of the circumstance of our previous encounter he replied,

"Well you're better at scoring goals than at nicking apples!" Then he added, "You're successful on the field because you take risks, I like that. But behind you here there is a whole team, both on and off the field, who will be with you and pulling for you all the time. You won't be left to shoulder responsibility alone."

It was a smart pitch, I signed for the club.

POWER POINT - *"Seek situations where the risk is minimal and/or shared and personal gain is substantial."*

When I entered into business I instinctively put into practice those same philosophies instilled in me. I deliberately sourced only the highest quality clients and colleagues to work with, those I could rely on and respect. I never exposed myself to a "You rob the bank, I'll run!" scenario which did not spread risk and share reward equitably between all.

Some people, when they become self-employed and go into business on their own account, are just too nice for their own good. They want too much to be pleasant to clients, customers, suppliers, staff, to all and sundry in fact. They want to be liked. They make the grave error of believing that if they are liked, then they will be successful. Not so.

While being liked is a significant element in the make up of a successful entrepreneur, that is all it is, an element. A far more important element is being tough and possessing the ability to say, "No!" It is precisely because they cannot say, "No!" that many self-employed business owners fail. These individuals do not stand up for themselves and state clearly what it is that they want. Because of that, such individuals do not earn respect. It's through respect that business success is achieved.

You're not in business to be popular and, even if you were, you'd never be popular with everyone. You're in business to win! It's competitive, cut throat. You're there to create a successful enterprise. It need not be beautiful to everyone, it need only be attractive to your chosen niche. Those outwith there may see you differently. Beauty truly is in the eyes of the beholder.

POWER POINT - *"You are not in business to be popular. Success comes from being respected."*

Once those to whom your credibility is important realise that you are not prepared to be pushed around or assume their responsibilities and liabilities, then they will respect you. Out of that respect will grow friendship and mutual trust.

You absolutely must let your public know exactly who you are, what you do and how you operate – this is often called branding. There is a great lack of clarity in much of the behaviour in present day society. People are not focussed. There is too much clutter in their lives and no real sense of purpose. When this is translated into the business arena it's a recipe for failure. You must be specific in your intentions and fully cognisant of exactly what you are trying to do and who you must engage with.

When you present yourself and your business in these open and honest ways, with integrity, then all those with whom it is important that you interact will respond in a similar vein. You will have no need to either rob a bank nor accept the responsibility for robbing one which you didn't!

Joseph T.Riach

Chapter 7

LOCATION, LOCATION, LOCATION

Unless your business is one which absolutely requires dedicated premises eg car repairs, carpentry work, undertaker, newsagent, restaurant etc. then the first option you'll certainly consider as to where to set up your enterprise is to work from your own home. There are many advantages. The first and most obvious is :

Cost – With no outlay on buying or renting of premises you are quids in to start with. You also save money by not having to commute to work, so no public transport and/or petrol to pay for, along with a saving on your general car running costs. You may not even need to keep a car?! Then there's the cost of clothes (you don't have to keep up appearances) and, of course, food .. no pricey eating out every day.

Then there's :

Time – Is more your own to do as you choose. In the morning you can sleep a little longer, go for a run, take a longer breakfast. You don't need to spend an age in the bathroom preparing for work and, as regards commuting, it's impossible to overestimate the sheer joy of not having to endure crowded trains or buses (and the depressing faces of the other frustrated and stressed out commuters) and the wasted hours of endless traffic jams with their unhealthy fumes. You do however need to manage your time well.

Comfort – Apart from the general comfort of being in the familiar setting of your own home with all your own things around you, you can just be relaxed and informal. No need for 'shirts and ties' or any special clothes, hair does or make up. Feel a cold coming on? Relax and stay cosy.

Flexibility – Work when you want, to your own rhythm. You maybe feel at your most productive in the morning or maybe you're a late at night type. It doesn't matter. You can fit in personal stuff like doctor or hairdresser appointments to suit yourself. Most importantly, you can enjoy more quality time with family and friends.

Life Balance - Apart from the family itself you feel closer to all aspects of your life when working from home (this even though you may well find yourself working more hours than you did when working for an employer). The autonomy of free decision making and release from forced structures and routines, reduces stress and creates time for healthy exercise and eating. You really do win all round.

… but … there can be disadvantages. Be aware of the -

Human Angle – Some people miss the interaction of working with others. They find it difficult to work without collaboration and validation. Is this you? On the other hand, be aware of lack of privacy. Around the house there can be unwelcome movement, distractions ... there are people. They may mean well but constant interruptions from family members or visitors with even just a 'harmless' "How are you getting on?" or "Would you like a coffee?" can be disruptive to concentration. Can you work in that environment? Is working from home right for you? You had better know. There are plenty of pros and cons. You must decide which ones are more important to you and which are likely to impact more on your well-being and happiness.

If you do decide to work from home then you really must possess these characteristics :

* Single Minded Concentration
* Relentless self-discipline
* Constant focus

and be able to

* Organise your workload
* Work unsupervised
* Structure your day
* Manage your time
* Be alone all day

Many people imagine that working from home is a casual affair, one not to be treated seriously. However, if considering your home as the commercial centre of your enterprise then it's a decision not to be taken lightly. In as much as operating your own business allows you the flexibility to choose your work location you should ensure that you operate in the environment which is most conducive to your calm and productivity.

Malcolm's Tale

Malcolm had worked as a senior executive for a leading oil exploration company for over thirty years when he was unceremoniously informed of his 'early retirement'. He was forty-eight years old.

But Malcolm was not a man easily fazed. He didn't lack self-confidence, possessed extensive industry knowledge and had good connections. He quickly decided to set up his own oil exploration consultancy.

His substantial terraced house near to the central business hub of the city, where he lived with his wife, teenage son and equally teenage daughter, three cats and Ben the family dog, became the centre for his new enterprise. His wife was thrilled at the prospect of having him at home every day. With her excited assistance, Malcolm reorganised the ground floor study at the front of the house to be his office. The door of the room opened on to the hallway immediately adjacent to the house's front entrance; ideal for restricting clients from any need to intrude further into the dwelling. The study had a large bay window facing on to the street and Malcolm sited his mahogany desk and leather swivel chair there. The whole set up delighted him and he opened for business.

His first day of operation went smoothly enough. He started work an hour later than he intended, having spent 'extra' time in bed, dallied over breakfast and watched the news on the television. The day was spent gazing at passers by on the street outside, broken occasionally by waves to and from people he knew, two long walks with Ben and a prolonged two hour lunch 'just this once'.

At six pm he concluded 'work' for the day exhausted ... and having established with certainty (three recounts) the exact number of paper clips which had accompanied him from his former office at the oil company. There were three hundred and twenty-seven of them.

The subsequent days, then weeks, then months followed a similar pattern. Oh yes, there were variations to his routine. These included – in no particular sequence and oft repeated –

his daughter throwing a noisy daytime party for her friends and his son returning the compliment with a drunken gathering of football hooligans; his wife offering him frequent cups of tea, coffee, 'something a little stronger' and highly annoying 'how is it going'? words of support; Ben demanding, lead in mouth and sad-eyed, to be walked; the cats taking it in apparently well organised turns to climb on every surface and scratch their grit and fur over every document in sight; strangers knocking on the window and 'speaking' to him in sign language; a steady stream of women's club members 'just popping their head in to say hello' as they passed to drink coffee with his wife in the kitchen at the back of the house; and no work getting done.

With each passing day Malcolm became more tired, more irritated and less productive. Soon the consultancy was in crisis. Something needed to be done.

He moved the study to the spare bedroom located immediately above the original office. This did deter the women's guild popping heads in brigade, but did nothing to allay the dog, cats, cups of tea and teenager interruptions. Nor did it deter the strangers passing outside who now threw pebbles to his window to catch his attention.

Next he relocated to the back bedroom. That solved the passer by problem … but now everything was so quiet! He could hear himself think – and he was doing a lot of that! Much more than he was doing work.

Eventually Malcolm decided that being in the house just wasn't working. He needed a 'real' place of work and he knew just the solution. His house, being a 'period' property, had an old coach house at the far end of the extensive garden. This was a two storey building which, in times gone by, had housed the proprietor's coach and horses with living accommodation on the upper floor for the chauffeur. More recently most of these buildings in neighbouring properties had been utilised as garages, stores, wash houses and workshops. Malcolm's was used as a garage for his car but now he set about renovating it to become a 'proper office'. Work completed he started work there. Things immediately improved.

Now he got up each morning on schedule as he had done previously while in employment. Then, after breakfast, he exited the back of the house by the kitchen door, marched the hundred yards to the coach house, unlocked what was the back door and let himself into his altogether more private and really rather professional office.

The 'office' fronted on to what was the main house's back lane and it was from there that clients and staff (Malcolm had hired a PA, both to help him out and also to add to the professional appearance of the business) entered. In the vastly improved ambience he felt more relaxed, more at home while being less at home, so to speak. His quality of work and productivity soon soared.

Still all was not well. His wife could still 'pester' him with endless cups of tea and coffee brought down the garden from the kitchen and his children, pets and other unwanted visitors could get to him the same way too.

Malcolm now decided that his real difficulty was that he missed going to work, as in making a journey to get there, and he needed to have only work space and only work people around him when he got there. He didn't want to commute, get on a bus or train or drive but he did feel that he needed to travel to work. He concluded that if he re-established his old going to work routine, then that would do the trick.

His next solution was to brick up the coach house door from the garden to his office as well as the coach house windows which looked out on to the garden. There was now no way to access the coach house from the main house and garden, nor for anyone to see into the coach house from there. The only access was via the lane.

Malcolm's new routine then became to leave for work each morning by his house's front door to walk the three-quarters of a mile along the main street, then the one hundred yards down the next road to the left and then the three-quarters of a mile back along the lane to the coach house. Once there he entered by the main, and only, door out on to the lane. It was perfect.

He enjoyed a half hour leg stretch in the morning, meeting people he knew along the way and calling in at the newsagent to pick up his daily journal. After work he could unwind with the return walk home and there were more than just a couple of welcoming pubs en route for him to stop off at for a drink before dinner.

In his office there was no Ben, no cats, no teenagers, no well-meaning wife, none of her friends and no passers-by to distract him. His PA opened the office, said "Good morning" to him when he arrived each day. She had all his various documents, calls and meetings arranged, brought him tea or coffee precisely when she knew he wanted it, never asked "How are things going?" and locked up after he left at night.

Quite suddenly all was very well!

Malcolm had found his perfect solution. Should you choose to work from home, you'll have to find yours.

Chapter 8

THE THREE OF ME

As a self-employed person I have always viewed my business as consisting of *three of Me* :

Me 1 is the owner or shareholder of the business. I set up the business as an investment for Me and to provide Me with income.

Me 2 is the MD (Managing Director) of the company. My role is to ensure the business runs effectively and profitably. I answer to the shareholder and I'm responsible for company planning and all operational aspects of the business, including -

Me 3 who is the sole employee of the company. I am responsible for day to day work and activity within the business. I answer to **Me 2**, the MD.

When **Me 2** does his job well he will ensure that the business remains healthy and he will motivate and support **Me 3**, including ensuring that discipline within the business is maintained eg. good time-keeping, impeccable standard of work, meticulous financial management, no waste - and no pilfering!

In simple terms, when the business is healthy it will be able to provide **Me 1** with a good investment and regular income. I look after the business, it looks after me!

If I don't look after the business well? ... then all three of me are stuffed!

This approach to practicing the management of self-employment in this manner is of course no different to the standard model which governs the successful stewardship of almost any business. An investor in the open market would want to invest in a sound company. That is a company which is :

- *Well established, a leader in its field*
- *Has a sought after product or service*
- *Possesses top quality management*
- *Experiences steady growth*
- *Has a strong customer base*
- *Is financially strong*
- *Has low or no debt*
- *And pays a good dividend*

That's what I want my company to be.

Were I a Managing Director of a company, I would want to know that I had investors behind me not looking for quick profit but who trust me to get on with the job of building the kind of company described above. I would have :

- *Pride in the company*
- *Confidence in my ability and professionalism*
- *A desire to establish the company as the best in the business*
- *And that's what I would want to be – the best in the business*

And were I an employee of a company, I would want :

- *To know that if I gave of my best that my efforts would be recognised, valued and rewarded*

- *That I had the trust of management and was seen as an important part of a team in which everyone was pulling in the same direction*

So the only difference between my 'self-employed company' and a bigger institution would be the fact that in the self-employed situation I must fulfill *all the roles* of the business – but hey! **that is quite some difference!**

It means that, not only is there no other personnel other than myself to perform the various tasks but, *crucially,* there is no other person to enforce the discipline required of me in conducting and enacting all aspects of the business. All the disciplines of work practice and of marketing and sales and of financial management and of every other of the myriad duties and activities involved in the day to day running of the business *must be imposed by myself on myself!*

POWER POINT - *"When self-employed, all the discipline inherent in running a successful business must be rigorously self-imposed."*

Get this factor right, the need for rigorous and constant self-discipline, and you will be well on the way to successful self-employment – *for all three of you!*

This discipline should include a Punishment and Reward element.

As a self-employed person I've long practiced the discipline of 'Punishment and Reward'. It's a simple and, in my view, necessary discipline if you work for yourself. It's no different after all than could be the case working for an employer who might, for instance, award you a bonus when you do well or might fire you for failure! When you are your own boss it is good practice to behave likewise.

Personally I've never felt so disenchanted with my own performance at work as to feel the need to fire myself (!) but I do punish myself in other ways when I feel I've under-performed. This might amount to denying myself a simple pleasure such as no wine with my dinner ... and with more serious failures no dinner at all! Or I might cancel time off for myself or a proposed trip abroad – yes I've done that!

On the other hand when I have a good day, close a sale, win a contract or complete a major project then I reward myself with restaurant visits, leisure breaks or foreign travel.

Yes, a punishment and reward policy helps to keep me focussed and motivated and to maintain a high level of performance. It's an essential part of any success strategy.

~

Business is a competitive pursuit. Make no mistake, it is a tough world, cut-throat even. No place for the fainthearted. But don't fret. It's not all blood and guts. You can compete without coming into direct conflict with others. Here's how.

* **First** remember that your biggest enemy is ... yourself! Overcoming that adversary is your biggest challenge. Win that battle and you'll win the war too. How come?

Well, it's all about being your best self in a business context. You must aim to be the best in the business. When you become that, in every respect, then your business will be the leader in it's field, the one the others are chasing. To get ahead, and stay ahead, you must :

* **Know** the market. Learn everything there is to learn about the industry/market in which you are trading. Become a specialist and an authority on the subject. This will not only give you a head start on your competitors, they will also come to you for guidance!

* **Know** your place in the market and how to establish and improve it. Plan, prepare and execute your business with diligence. Every area of your business must be honed to perfection. That will include evaluating in depth some or all of the following disciplines, departments, activities and practices -

Accounting and financial management, legal and compliance, sales, manufacturing, operations, transportation, marketing and branding, personnel and human resources, purchasing, customer relations, communications and technology ... and more

- and taking appropriate action to make them efficient, effective and best in class.

* **Know** your competitors – inside out! Having looked inwards at the competitor who is yourself, you must look outwards at the competition in the wider market. The good news is that this need not be a 'direct contact sport'. Yes, it can be likened to a boxing match or an athletics race, but there's an easier way than indulging in the equivalent of physical confrontation. It's really rather simple.

What you do is to repeat the exercise of analysing and equating every aspect of your competitor's business in exactly the same way, and in the same detail, as you evaluated all the processes of your own business. In this way you can know

your enemy even more intimately than he knows himself!
Then you can lay your own plans and act accordingly.

First look within. Then look with the same eyes outwith.
Act on what you see. That is how to win in business.

POWER POINT - *"Look within, look outwith, act on what you see."*

One thing you should never do in business is speak badly
of other businesses. Especially your direct competition and
those working in the same field as yourself. Don't 'trash the
competition'! Such an approach will succeed only in
discrediting yourself. Why?

Firstly - In promoting your business, your focus must be
on what you can do and what you do well, not on what
someone else can't do or does badly.

Secondly - It brings into question your own integrity. If
you are seen and heard to speak badly of a third party, what
might you be saying to others about the person or client you
are addressing your remarks to?

Thirdly - It is negative behaviour and will be recognised as
such. People do not do business with negative individuals.
They respond to upbeat and positive overtures.

Fourthly - When your opposition are lacking in certain
aspects of their business or comportment then a savvy client
will find out anyway. Let the source of the 'bad news' be
someone other than yourself.

Even in the event that a client brings up himself failings or
shortcomings in a competitor and asks for your verification,
view or opinion on the matter do not get sucked into vilifying
them. Apart from other considerations you could be guilty of

defamation. That aside, it is best that you sidestep any criticisms of your opposition. Better by far to say something nice or complimentary about them instead; that will earn you respect.

At the very least, do not comment. Restrict conversation to the industry in general and redirect it towards the benefits which you and your enterprise have to offer.

POWER POINT - *"Don't trash the competition. Focus on, and speak about, what you do well."*

Your client will soon come to realise that your greatest selling point is that you are a person of integrity. One to be trusted and one whose discretion can be relied upon. He'll know you and like you for it. He'll respect all three of you!

Joseph T.Riach

Chapter 9

BUDGET FOR SUCCESS

There are many people in business who are successful at making money but not very good at holding on to it! In other words they lack the ability to control their spending. While creating income is the first requisite of becoming wealthy, you must keep hold of as much of the money that you make as possible in order to stay wealthy. In order to do that it is necessary to create and implement a budget. A budget is a forecast of your proposed future spending which you intend to adhere to. Simple in theory, less so in practice, because the first requirement of good budgeting is ... self-discipline.

POWER POINT - *"To operate an effective budget takes restraint and strong self-discipline."*

The second requirement is that you must write down your financial plan, your budget. As with all business plans unless it is first put in writing then there is no plan. Where to start?

First off, segment the coming financial year into months, weeks and days on your budget chart or spreadsheet. You're going to control your annual spending by reducing it to manageable smaller periods. I work on a daily basis.

The next thing is to forecast how much your spending is going to be. There are two ways to calculate this.

The first is to look at your spending over the past and previous years and then, working from that, calculate which expenditures will recur, increase, decrease or not occur in the coming year; what additional expenses might arise and which ones you could actually eliminate.

The second way to calculate your spending is simply to start with a clean slate and think of every conceivable expense and then some more which your business could incur over the coming year. Include an amount for unforeseen expenses, contingencies. This should give you an absolute 'top line' for expenditures which throughout the year should provide opportunities to save money against your budgeted figure.

Saving against budget is what you should strive for whichever method you have used to calculate your budget.

I personally calculate using both methods then I compare them and generally arrive at a projection which is a cross between the two. Whatever my conclusion, my aim is always in operation for my actual expenditure to come in under budget. At every turn, on a day to day basis, I try to under-cut my estimated expenditures or not incur them at all. That is the art of operating an effective budget. Yes, it does require discipline and restraint.

Of course expenditures will not all fall into regular daily or weekly patterns on your budget chart. Some might arise every day, others on the same day each week or month but there will also be one-off payments which only fall due on one specific date in the year.

So it's important to know not just what money is going to go out ... but when. That's where *Cash Flow* comes in!

Cash flow, as the title implies, refers to the movement of money in and out of your business. You will hopefully have forecast and be expecting that revenues for your business will be greater than your outgoings and therefore creating lovely profit for you. But ... if your expenditures predate your income then you're going to be in a negative cash flow situation i.e. you will be spending money that you don't yet have! That means that you will need to dip into capital or savings, borrow money or run up a bank overdraft while waiting for inward revenues to arrive. Not good!

Your aim should be to always maintain a positive cash flow. So set up your business in such a way that you always have money coming in first, then out second! Find ways to ensure that this is the case because if you can't then you're probably not in the right business. The idea of having an enterprise is, after all, to make money, not to incur debt.

Having your clients or customers pay you up front before you supply your goods or services is the best strategy (and their payments can be arranged on direct debit or bank transfer). That way they are financing your business for you and ensuring a positive cash flow.

POWER POINT - *"Ensure a positive cash flow for your enterprise by having clients or customers pay in advance for your goods or services."*

Draw up your budget forecast clearly projecting not only all expenditures but also all earnings; and not only the amounts but also the dates. Then, where-ever possible, adjust expenditures to later dates and earnings to earlier dates. Get as much money as possible coming in as quickly as possible. Have money going out as little and as slowly as possible. That is the art of successful – and profitable – budgeting!

One of the surest way to have money coming in before it

goes out is to employ the *'Sell First, Buy Second'* strategy. Yes you read that right. Always sell before you buy.

Do you find that odd? Do you perhaps think that it's a typographical error and that it should read "Buy first, then sell?" That after all is the sequence that people usually follow, buy something and then sell it. But no, this is no error. I have quite deliberately written 'Sell First, Buy Second'. The question is, "Why?"

For the answer we must first go back to my oft quoted observations about success and successful people. I have written that to 'think successful' takes a certain mindset. Given that only a very small percentage of people are 'successful' and wealthy – 5% of the population, no more – it follows that only this select group have the 'right' attitude in this context. Therefore it also follows that everyone else's attitude in this context is the 'wrong' attitude.

This is a very important point indeed. It means that the opinions and ideas of Ninety Five Per Cent of the population, as espoused daily on television, in the pub and in the workplace are totally worthless. They may make up 95% of opinion but they **make up 100% of unsuccessful opinion!** The ideas and practices of the Five Per Cent on the other hand **make up 100% of successful, entrepreneurial opinion.** These very success ideas and practices will be totally alien to what 'Joe Public' thinks contributes to success.

POWER POINT - *"Learn to think like one of the 5% and accept that you will be different from 'Joe Public'."*

With the "Sell and then Buy principle" we have the most profound, specific example of how a 5%er thinks and acts differently from anyone else. In fact, what I am about to reveal to you is one of *the single most profound 'secrets' of the super successful!* Here it is :

"5%ers do not Buy then Sell. 5%ers only ever Sell then Buy!"

POWER POINT - *"Successful entrepreneurs never buy then sell, they first sell and then buy!"*

The simple sense of the sell then buy philosophy is so powerful that it totally goes over the head of the majority of the populace. If presented to them most will question how it can be. Surely you must buy something before you can sell it? How can you sell something which you don't already own?

Of course the answer to both of these questions is that it's perfectly possible to first sell and then to buy something but to understand the practice you must first develop the mindset and attitude of a 5%er.

Remember, very successful people generally follow very simple wealth creation practices. So simple in fact that the majority of people cannot see or will not believe that these practices are at the very heart of the 5%er's success.

POWER POINT - *"Successful entrepreneurs follow such simple wealth creation practices that the majority of people cannot see or will not believe that these practices are at the very heart of their success."*

No-one wants to or sets out to make a loss in business but what 5%ers do is to ensure that the risk of loss is negligible. Therefore they develop practices which absolutely minimise the risk of loss while hugely increasing the likelihood of profit. The Sell then Buy approach is one of their most powerful tactics. It gives the practitioner two huge but simple benefits.

You need never make a loss

You need never hold stock

Selling first means that a sale price is established only if it exceeds the known cost of acquiring the article and that, in turn, means that there is never any need to buy anything or to hold stock. What, after all, is the point of incurring the cost of buying, storage, staff costs and transportation when someone else will bear it? *Let someone else take the risk.*

By the same token it is wiser by far to work on commissions rather than buy/sell stock. Better earn $1 million and keep it all as profit rather than turn over $20 million with all the attendant hassle and cost to make the same $1 million. Simple!

POWER POINT - *"Never buy anything until you have already sold it at a higher price. That way you will always make money."*

To reiterate and emphasise. Never buy anything until you have already sold it at a higher price. Sell then buy. That way you *will always make money.* Just like the super rich.

BOOK 2

ACTION!

Small Steps For Giant Gains

Joseph T.Riach

Chapter 10

THE FREEWAY TO PROFIT

Whatever mankind has ever set out to do, having once done it he then looks for ways to do it better. It's an absolute law of our creation. Doing it better means producing a superior end result whilst achieving that result more easily and at less cost in terms of labour, finance or both. The finest example ever is the invention of the wheel.

The wheel revolutionised how man does just about everything. From its humble basic origin it has evolved into a sophisticated implement which impacts on every area of our lives. Its countless incarnations are all technically vastly superior to the original but they are produced easily and cheaply by modern production methods. In other words we now get from the wheel infinitely greater benefits than ever but more easily than ever.

Earning a living is no different. It is perfectly clear that any sane person should want to achieve life's maximum rewards for as little effort as possible. This is a totally understandable, ethical and moral ambition. There is nothing wrong with wanting this. I believe that self-employment provides the best opportunity to realise this ideal.

But I was brought up to believe in the 'Victorian work ethic' and in a strict presbyterian culture to boot. Deep in my psyche were sown the seeds of 'hard work is good for the soul' and other dire dogma of the time. Not that I don't believe to this day that hard work is central to success. It is, but I also believe that **working smart is critical**. The ultimate pie-in-the-sky ideal earning-wise would be to do absolutely nothing at all while pocketing millions of dollars each and every day! That of course is unrealistic, wishful thinking. Yet there is nothing wrong with trying to get as near to such a goal as possible. It is in my entrepreneurial and self-employed existence that I have achieved just that. I have employed a 'more money for less effort' methodology to great effect and which is ridiculously simple.

It wasn't always so. In the beginning I had to learn all about the self-employment strategies which this book is all about. Once 'out on my own' I learned quickly.

The first and most important thing that I learned is that to make an 'easy' gain it is necessary to buy and sell, or more significantly to sell and buy, something. Labour, and by that I mean working manually or mentally a set number of hours, day in day out, will never make you seriously wealthy.

POWER POINT - *"Real wealth is created by buying and selling, or selling then buying, something. Labour, working a set number of hours day after day, year after year, will never make you rich."*

It's also important that you learn to sell and buy something which is the easiest something to sell and buy. Something which yields good profit but with limited risk. Were I asked to draw up a blueprint of what I considered to be the perfect object to sell and buy in order to 'easily' make regular, attractive profits, then I would say that it would have to be something which -

* I could always sell or buy readily

* Should have the potential for big profit
* Have limited downside risk
* No holding of stock
* No physical movement of goods

There are many businesses which can be run in such a way as to meet these criteria. What you must do is find and/or set up your business so as to conform to these rules. Settle for nothing less. The principles can be applied to virtually any business. It is not the specific trade or profession which you choose which matters most. *It is how you create and run your business that is key. Create it to meet your needs.*

~

Do you know what the initials O.P.M. stand for? They stand for *Other People's Money.* If you are truly serious about becoming wealthy, then you should give some thought to O.P.M. Why? Because, if it were possible to use other people's money rather than your own in order to succeed in self-employment then that wouldn't be too bad an idea would it? In fact it's the very method used by successful entrepreneurs since time immemorial! They've been at it for generations.

POWER POINT - *"Generations of entrepreneurs have used other people's money rather than their own in order to create great wealth."*

Now before you go out to rob a bank, let's make it clear that Other People's Money in the context to which we are referring here means legally accessed money. OK, where does one get O.P.M. legally?

The most common form of O.P.M. which people have

access to is a loan. The first place to ask for a loan is of friends and relatives. Many enterprises and personal fortunes have been built from capital first borrowed from family members or from friends.

POWER POINT - *"Many enterprises and personal fortunes have been built from capital first borrowed from friends or relatives."*

The next place to go for a loan, which all people have access to, is a bank. A loan from a bank is effectively O.P.M. The bank is simply lending out their depositors' money at a higher rate of interest than that which they are paying to the depositors. Of course it's not always easy to convince your bank to lend you the money for your proposed enterprise so it's essential to draw up detailed plans and costings. In fact you should always do this regardless of whom you are asking the money from.

There are also Crowd Funding Platforms, Venture Capital Companies and 'Business Angels' (private individuals and investors) prepared to put up capital to finance ventures. Find them and ask them. The worst that can happen is that they say, "No."

Another example of O.P.M. at work, and a superbly effective strategy, is the use of a publicly listed limited liability company (PLC). With a PLC the operation is funded at the shareholders' expense, while the founders and operators have only limited risk. In a PLC the company founders raise money by selling shares in the company to the public. So the company is capitalised and the company's activities supported by the use of O.P.M. In the event that the company fails, the loss is borne by the shareholders. But when the company prospers then not only do the shareholders gain, but so too do the company founders.

Another way to capitalise your business and to give it a positive cash flow is to have your clients pay in advance for the goods or services you are supplying. In my role of business consultant/trouble shooter and when reviewing systems within client businesses, I inevitably recommend that they adopt such a prepay policy for all of their customers.

Initially, this suggestion is almost always met with resistance if not outright hostility. Typical responses from business owners range from,

"That won't work in this business or this industry," to my own particular favourite,

"We'll lose half of our clients!"

To which my standard response is,

"No! You'll lose *all* of your non-payers!"

Most businesses do come to see the benefit of such an arrangement and will go for it.

Therefore anyone with serious intentions of building wealth simply must give consideration to the use of O.P.M. and endeavour to find ways to exploit it. The principle of using O.P.M. is a philosophy long applied by the wealthy and the serious entrepreneur will always seek ways to finance his wealth creation activities at someone else's expense rather than his own. It is a terrific way of reducing risk and liability?

POWER POINT - *"The use of other people's money to create wealth is an important risk management strategy."*

So, never incur any cost that you don't have to. Where a cost must be incurred try to find ways of reducing it, including trying to pass the cost on to someone else.

Should you borrow money only do so in circumstances where you can be 'certain' of creating a substantially bigger sum of money than that borrowed and where you can be certain of paying back the borrowed capital quickly.

Never go in for 'dead' borrowing. Dead borrowing is any situation where you borrow money other than to make money e.g. mortgage, car loan, holiday loan – these all eat up money, cost a fortune and make you poorer. Those who go in for 'dead' borrowing generally become less well off because of it rather than wealthy!

To recap, borrow only to spend on ventures which will reasonably certainly create a profit greater than the sum borrowed, and quickly. Analyse the Risk/Reward Ratio! Then, if it shows a very good potential profit against a low risk – go for it!

As before stated, many of the most renowned entrepreneurs and successful business giants of this and previous centuries originally financed their ventures with O.P.M. Sometimes from a bank or financial institution but often from friends and acquaintances. Often in fact from complete strangers!

Thus the moral is – Don't be afraid to ask! Ask anyone and everywhere. Pride should not come into it. The worst that can happen is that you can be refused. On the other hand, if you ask, then you might be accepted. Take the risk of being successful!

POWER POINT - *"The only risk you take in asking for financial assistance is the risk of being successful!"*

Of course, have a sound plan prepared and documented, backed up by research and information. You will then be able to substantiate to your proposed backer that what you have to offer is a well thought out venture and that you yourself are credible and trustworthy. You must demonstrate that your proposal is sound and profitable in its own right. Remember, you may also be competing for this money against other proposals put to the backer so your proposition must be better than any others and also be the best presented.

POWER POINT - *"Always do your homework. Prepare meticulously."*

When successful, repay promptly. In this way your personal credibility soars. Then you will find it progressively easier to raise finance from many different sources. In fact, when your credibility and reputation are high, offers of money will come to you as if by magic and from places you would never have imagined. You will find yourself having to vet the sources rather than the other way round. That's when you know that you've really arrived as an entrepreneur to be reckoned with!

~

Another thing to ask for as well as money, are items or goods which could assist you or your business. I call these F.O.C. items. Something which comes your way Free of Charge is often as good as cash in hand. It's amazing what people and businesses run out of a use for or simply discard. Ask them before they do chuck the stuff. What is surplus and useless to one person could be invaluable to you!

POWER POINT - *"Ask for free of charge items or goods. What is surplus and useless to one person could be* *invaluable to you."*

If you are in business shop around for F.O.C. items. Also try to make the business self-financing. By that I mean, don't use your own capital or borrowed money but rather use your customers' or clients' money. O.P.M. in other words! How? Well cash businesses are best. That's where people pay you cash up front for goods or services. There's no waiting for weeks or even months for invoices to be settled. Your customers' money runs your business rather than your own resources being drained.

POWER POINT - *"A positive cash-flow cuts out the need for borrowing or the use of your own capital."*

If providing a service, arrange for your clients to pay you by monthly subscription on bankers direct debit. That way you have a positive cash flow from day one and know exactly how much money is coming in each month and when. Often you will be **getting paid ahead of actually doing the work** – always the best policy. Your clients will also appreciate the easy payment method with no big bill to shock them at some future date. Everyone wins!

If dealing in goods it's best not to stock them. That ties up cash. Best is to **sell before you buy** or arrange payment on a commission basis from your supplier - even if it means taking a smaller mark up. Either way have your supplier deliver directly to your customer. Then you'll never incur transportation, storage nor handling charges.

Where money owed to you is a problem, look at what goods or items your creditor may have that could be of value to you. I've collected vehicles, office equipment and tools in the past. Oh! and quite a few meals! Who says there's no such thing as a free dinner!?

A good F.O.C. arrangement gets you paid, saves you stress, gets the other guy off the hook. It thereby creates good will AND it often leads to profit when moving stuff on.

No road to ruin for you. Only the freeway to profit!

Joseph T.Riach

Chapter 11

WINNING WAYS

Understanding and practicing the success secrets of self-employed super achievers is essential to success in business. Their winning ways are not always easy to comprehend nor to implement but in many other instances their concepts are ridiculously simple. Whichever the case it is essential if set on success to follow their example. Their practices, once taken on board, will change your life forever.

Having a high public profile is, contrary to some opinion not a necessary requisite of becoming or being successful. Of course many hugely wealthy people are consistently in the public eye and thrive on it. At least an equal number however maintain a low profile and are effectively invisible to the outside world. These last are probably the smarter ones. They let others bask in the limelight but stay themselves well below the parapet.

For many, not being in the 'firing line' gives them a big advantage in the entrepreneurial stakes. With some their anonymity extends to not having debt, not owning property nor cars and, in fact, not having their name appear on documents nor anywhere. They are completely invisible and as such able to fully enjoy the benefits of their wealth, free from stress or conflict. They adhere to the maxim of,

"Let others take the heat ... I'll take the profit!" Think about it!

They also create their own perfect business to match the criteria which suits them. They don't let the business dictate to them. This is extremely important. Who wants to be slave to their business? Might as well be working for an employer. Smart entrepreneurs design their business around their wants. For me, that 'perfect business' is defined as :

• *It must be self-financing* - That means no capital outlay on my part, no borrowing, a positive cash flow from minute one and it operates on other people's money and with free of charge items

• *There should be no employees, premises or goods*

• *It must generate maximum income from least effort,*

That's the challenge!

POWER POINT - *"The perfect business should produce the maximum income from the least effort."*

To find the perfect business you mustn't just start up in any old business. Instead design your business around your desires of the lifestyle you want rather than letting your business dictate to you.

Many businessmen and women get into businesses that consume vast amounts of their time and energy and turn over huge amounts of money but make little profit. These businesses tend to control the owner(s) rather than the owner(s) driving the business. The enterprise is not meeting the owners real wants.

You can create a 'monster' which creates vast wealth but which consumes just as much and burns up your precious lifetime and energy with it. Isn't it better to turn over a smaller amount of money for little effort yet have the vast bulk of that money as your own, as clear profit? And to have time to enjoy it? Lots of employees can give you lots of help, they can also cause you endless hassle and cost you a fortune. You don't want employees or expensive premises, factories, warehouses or goods to move. You want something simple!

As regards learning about simple working, there is no substitute for real life experience. Sometimes this can take the form of time spent in the company of someone who possesses wisdom which you lack. From the countless such encounters which have featured heavily in my life and thus helped shape my destiny, following are two of the most significant. Each experience, innocuous though it might seem at first glance, literally changed my life. Who knows, reading of them might change your life too ..... ?

What Is The Difference - Experience 1.

The flamboyant and garrulous business magnate was holding court in his favourite west end wine bar surrounded by an adoring throng of young wannabe entrepreneurs. He pointed dramatically to the car park where sat his brand new Mercedes coupe, conspicuous among the ragtaggle of second hand Fords, Fiats and other dilapidated minor marques which surrounded it.

"Tell me guys," he demanded loudly, goading his prey, "Tell me what is the difference between my super Mercedes Benz top of the range luxury limousine gleaming out there and your sad and poxy beat up heaps of scrap? Look outside, look at them, tell me what is the difference?"

Silence followed, accompanied by shuffling of feet and puzzled glances while the great man eyed his audience, a wide mischievous smile bridging his jaw. At last one young hopeful coughed nervously and ventured the obvious,

"Well your car is a Mercedes and mine isn't."

"No it isn't a Mercedes is it?" the top man scolded, "It isn't even close is it? But I'll tell you something else that your car isn't. Would you like to know what that something is young man?"

The junior swallowed hard and stumbled out a dry-throated, "Well … er … yes, what *isn't* my car?"

"Well for starters it isn't a car," roared the reply, "That rust-bucket is a disgrace to the very word, but I'll tell you something else that it isn't … it isn't paid for!"

A pause. "Well I'm right aren't I?"

A begrudging nod of agreement.

"And I'll tell you all one other thing and I guarantee that I'm 100% right; there's not one of those deplorable apologies for wheels out there which is not on credit, you're all paying them up at some exorbitant cost … and then … then you're borrowing on top of that again to make ends meet. I'm right aren't I?"

Not one voice was raised in dissent; most present looked downward and felt kind of ashamed.

Now, with the full attention of all secured, the magnate continued,

"Now look at my Mercedes Benz limousine, look at the bonnet (hood), what do you see there?"

Everyone quickly agreed that the famous three-pointed star was the object of his question and they were in fact correct.

"But," he carried on, "Do you know what the three points of the star stand for? I'll bet you don't, so I'll tell you. The three points of the star stand for," and here he spelled it out, slow and clear,

"Paid .... In .... Cash!"

With that he slammed his fist on the table causing all present to jump and some to tremble,

"And THAT gentlemen is the difference – now do you get it?"

I was that young man mentioned and yes I did get it. Within twelve months I was free of all borrowing and to this day I have never again had personal credit of any kind.

POWER POINT - *"Size doesn't matter!! 'Paid for' does!"*
What Is The Difference? - Experience 2.

"This place doesn't suit my life style," I confessed to Antonio, my Portuguese real estate agent friend as we relaxed over an outrageously long lunch of open-fire grilled sardines and an unwise volume of vinho verde. He drew heavily on his untipped Gitanes Brune and sized me up from narrowed eyes behind his Ray Ban wraparounds.

"No my friend," a hiss of blue smoke accompanied his words, "You are wrong. It is your life style which does not suit this place."

That made me think.

We were seated at a rough wooden table, on an equally vulgar wooden veranda which reached on to a golden sand beach and flirted with the emerald sea beyond. Fernando's tin-shack restaurant would not have survived even a cursory glance from any self-respecting environmental health inspector. Yet it was, and is, one of the finest restaurants at which I have ever eaten.

Fresh fish and seafood to die for, prices so low that the restaurant is almost paying you to dine there, jolly camaraderie as from a bygone age and a vista of deeply sublime tranquility. In short - Paradise!

"The difference between you and I," Antonio continued, "Is this. If I were to sell a villa in the morning, I would shut up the office and go home to my wife and children. We would prepare a picnic basket of presunto hams and cheeses, home baked bread, garlic and olives, fresh tomatoes, figs and basil, almond cake and lots of lemonade and wine and we'd go to the beach. We would stay there and away from my work for as long as it pleased us."

With the sun on my brow and the sea breeze caressing my cheeks it was not at all difficult for me to fall in with his typically Portuguese, laissez-faire view of life. The truth is that, at that moment, such a laid back life style was already sounding totally logical.

"You on the other hand!" his raised voice drew me from the idyllic trance threatening to kidnap me, "You," he repeated accusingly, "If you were to sell a villa in the morning, you would come back in the afternoon and try to sell another one. You know how to work but you don't know how to live. I," ... and here he spiraled his index finger upward with a dramatic Latin flourish ... , "I know of life. And THAT my friend is the difference between you and I."

This conversation took place many years ago and it did indeed make me think. So much so that not long afterwards I took the decision to relocate abroad permanently and with it radically change my life style. It is by far and away the best thing I have ever done. Now, most days, I relax with local amigos over outrageously long lunches of grilled fresh fish and insane volumes of vinho tinto, consumed at provocatively romantic tin-shack beach restaurants. And, were I in the real estate business (which I'm not), I swear that I would never never ever, even remotely consider trying to sell a second villa in the afternoon had I already sold one in the morning!

You see, today I live and 'work' in the sunny south of Portugal. Need I say more?

POWER POINT - *"A debt free and care free life is there for the taking. Just do it!"*

Debt free equals care free. Live life for today but also appreciate that the power of money is in having it.

When you have money you possess the ability to influence people and circumstances in ways not possible when you have none. Spending it gives away that power. It is absolutely crucial to understand the simple fact that the real power of money lies in having it … not spending it.

After all having lots of money equals 'choice' and 'power' and with those you can achieve and possess anything and everything you might ever desire - and without spending any money! So, when you make money – hold on to it. Don't incur debt but do relax and enjoy your wealth too. Learn to live!

Joseph T.Riach

Chapter 12

WHY TAKE THE RISK?

Whether self-employed, in business or just going about your daily life, you are regularly taking risks of some kind. But not all of you evaluate situations methodically and learn how to manage risk. Those who do, give yourselves an advantage. You realise that, be it simply crossing the road, deciding on an every-day purchase or perhaps taking part in a sporting activity, risk is involved. Then you weigh up the prospective reward against the potential loss.

POWER POINT - *"There's risk of some kind involved in everything you do in life, whether you like it or not!"*

With 'Risk Management' all that you're considering is to make sure that you know what the risk is in any given situation and to evaluate if you are prepared to afford it (the risk). The risk of crossing the road for instance, where there is no pedestrian crossing but several lanes of heavy traffic, is high risk. You could be hit by a vehicle and lose your life.

The risk of buying the latest technology gadget is less. It might not function as you wish or could overstretch your budget leaving you short of cash for a period, but it won't kill you. There you have two extremes.

Whatever the situation there is a simple test you can always apply to help you evaluate risk. It's a simple question. It's my favourite question and I apply it all the time. The question is, "*Why take the risk?*"

POWER POINT - *"One of the most powerful tools at your disposal in 'Risk Management' or in just running your life is the simple question – Why Take The Risk?"*

You see, when you predetermine the extent of the loss you are prepared to incur in any situation – be it the loss of your life or of a few hundred dollars – then you can limit your risk to just that amount. Hence the term '*Limited Risk*'. i.e. you limit your risk to the predetermined amount (in these examples, your life or a few hundred dollars). From that you can decide what your '*Risk Exposure*' will be.

Risk Exposure refers to how much you are prepared to lose in order to expose yourself to the potential gain. The next relevant question being, "What is the potential gain?" Evaluating the risk against the potential gain is called the *Risk/Reward Ratio.* Ideally you want the risk to be low and the potential reward to be high.

POWER POINT - *"Evaluating the risk against the potential gain is called the Risk/Reward Ratio. Ideally the risk should be low and the potential reward high."*

The ideal may not always be achievable but the principle holds good. In practice, you should always ensure that you are looking at a healthy potential reward in relation to a lowish risk. That is clearly not the case in the crossing-the-road example cited. That's maximum risk for no purpose. But it could well be the case when investing in the new technology purchase. Lots of potential benefits with downside risk limited to a few hundred dollars. Getting the balance right is the trick!

In many situations, if the risk is negligible then the likelihood is that the reward will be low also. And if the reward is very high then the risk is likely to be great. What high achievers, that small proportion of the populace who over-achieve, have learned to do is to sway the odds in their favour. They have learned to consistently lower the risk while increasing the potential gain from their commercial or other activities. They have done this in an infinite variety of ways, using ploys and tactics learned through practice and experience.

One sure-fire way already highlighted is to sell first and then buy - equals zero risk and name your profit!

Whatever their practices, all contain two vital elements. Can you guess what they are? Yes, that's right - *'Simple'* and *'Repeat'*. Risk management strategies of super achievers are always remarkably simple and are carried out repetitively!

POWER POINT - *"Simple strategies carried out repetitively and well add up to great achievements."*

Entrepreneurs of course take risks, that is the essential characteristic that defines them. But the smart and successful ones manage their risk. What seems a risky situation to others will have been carefully assessed by them. They take only limited risk, never exposing themselves to potential loss beyond their predetermined extent of acceptable loss. They evaluate risk/reward carefully. They always ask, "Why take the risk?" So too should you.

Note also that risk is not a purely mathematical issue. It has other dimensions too. These can include psychological, social, and political factors. There is no mathematical formula to tell any of you whether to take a chance on starting a business, proposing marriage, or riding a bicycle on city streets. You must weigh up the possible outcomes and then commit to a course of action, **in the knowledge that the future is uncertain and unknown..**

You can be led by data. But data is a sextant, not a destination. What are you being led towards? What level of risk are you prepared to accept? What are you prepared to sacrifice to reduce that risk? These questions are not statistical, but inherently personal.

Ask yourself, "What kind of risk are you willing to take and for what purpose?" Remember - **Zero-risk life is not an option!**

~

My home town football team had qualified for their first cup final appearance in many years. On the day of the 'big match', I excitedly headed for the stadium. En route I stopped at a pub for one or three pre-game beers. I struck up a conversation with some fans of the opposing team. In the course of the light-hearted banter between us it emerged that these fellows had all placed bets on 'my team' to win. Puzzled, I asked, "Why?" Their revelation would prove to be, quite literally, life changing.

"Easy," I was told, "Of course we want our boys to win, that will make us very happy. But, if your team should happen to win, then we can drown our sorrows off the profit from our winning bets. Either way we win!"

Such simple logic! On the one hand they'd win emotionally, on the other they'd gain financially. A true win-win situation. Why didn't I think of that?

Well, after that I did think about it - a lot - and, in the interim, I have put the strategy into practice regularly. The result being that sometimes I've enjoyed the emotional euphoria of 'my favourites' winning, while on other occasions the pain of their defeat has been assuaged by a compensatory pay out from my 'friendly neighbourhood bookmaker'! Win-win indeed. So much so in fact that I soon took to wondering how I might be able to apply the same principle to life generally and to my business endeavours in particular?

More so, how might I ensure that I won on both counts, emotionally and financially? and all the time - yes, I wanted it all ways! The solutions I came up with (there are several) are, of course, remarkably simple.

Key to them all is ... *first and foremost in life, set out to help people, be it in small or in meaningful ways.* Always do that and you'll always be emotionally satisfied. With that requirement established there only remains the, "How to ensure financial gain while doing it?" question.

Well, when you help people, be it personally or in a business context, many will instinctively want to help you. They'll want to return the kindness shown to them. Some will offer you gifts; accept graciously. Others will inquire as to what you do in life, how you earn your living. Only reveal that when asked. Then, when your goods or services are ones that they want and can afford, you'll be able to assist them further and enjoy personal gain too by supplying their needs.

Even if you are not a provider of what they ask for, know someone who is and who will pay you a commission. Or source what they want anyway. It's extra earning for you and might turn out to be the gateway to a new enterprise. Either way, the recipient of your original kindness will want to deal with you and will be happy to have you benefit from their purchase.

When you employ the 'help others' strategy in this way, you experience both emotional and financial gain. You eliminate all risk from the 'bet'. There is no reckless risk, there is not even calculated risk. There is only what I call 'controlled non-risk'. You set up and control the situation, therefore you ensure the outcome. It's guaranteed win-win. Wait - it gets better!

It turned out that my new friends had financed their entire day out by organising the day and hiring the coach for the trip. They had divided the cost of the hire between the other forty plus travellers so that their own transport was free. They had also added a mark up on top of that to cover their spending. This included their bets! They had eliminated all cost and with it any financial risk. Their entire day out was 'free'.

It may only have been a football match, only a few beers and a laugh. But the lesson I learned that cup final day far surpassed the pleasure of winning. Yes, 'my' team did win the cup – great joy. The opposition fans won too. They collected on their winning bets. I have much to thank them for. They showed me how to create and control win-win situations. They were veritable entrepreneurs. They were smart fellows!

They taught me the 'Never and Always' principle which you'll see referred to in several guises within this book -

Never pay for anything. Always get paid up front.

~

You'll also reduce risk in running your business when you factor into your operation what I call *'The Shelf Life Principle'.*

This basically lays down that everything that you do and everyone that you deal with has a limited time span within which they are fully effective and/or of maximum value. When that time has passed then they must be discarded and/or replaced. It's critical for the success of your enterprise to :

•**Know when that time is imminent**

and

•**Act decisively without fear or favour**

The optimum period of time in question will of course vary from just a few weeks in some instances to many, many years in others. As regards employees for instance, I have parted company with more than just a few within hours, days or weeks, many after only a year or two. While others of genuine commitment and value to myself or my enterprises were with me throughout my career. The crucial thing is to be able to differentiate between quality worth persevering with and those whose futures would be better catered for elsewhere.

The same applies as regards clients, contracts, projects and suppliers. Some (hopefully all or many) will have shelf lives as long as your own professional life. But all need constant review and some will not be of benefit kept on board beyond a certain point. They have to go. This itself is a policy of review and renewal and creates space for fresh, more appropriate opportunities to be pursued and to occupy your time and efforts.

There is also the question of growth. Expansion of your enterprise must not come at the cost of retaining unproductive personnel or unprofitable clientele whose presence is paid for by new and rewarding projects. Retaining bodies or contracts just to make up the numbers is never a good idea. Better to do without as regards staff until people of the right pedigree are available; and the same applies to enterprises which have outlived their usefulness.

Work your employees and your contracts to the maximum benefit of all, while you can. But be aware that people and circumstances change, not always for the better, and that a parting of ways will in many cases become inevitable. Remember, you're not in business to be liked, so bite the bullet and do the necessary.

Apart from trying to be just too damned likeable to those who you really need to rid yourself of, there are other reasons that can cause your business venture to fall by the wayside. The mistakes entrepreneurs make are mostly incredibly simple, so simple in fact that it may be hard to comprehend how anyone coming into business could possibly fall into the traps. But they do – all the time!

The two biggest failures are :

An inability to create sales

and

Poor money management

Yes, simple but true. Not getting enough cash coming in and failing to look after it properly when it does are the single biggest killers of fledgling businesses.

POWER POINT - *"Concentrate your efforts on sales and money management. Negligence of these are the biggest killers to businesses."*

These faults themselves derive from one big failing on the part of the budding entrepreneur. And that is :

The lack of a properly assessed business plan with ongoing oversight and management.

Generally speaking, those entrepreneurs with good plans, soundly managed and regularly assessed, do not experience the lack of sales and money management difficulties which can prove to be terminal for many. There are though, other common pitfalls. While I much prefer to concentrate on success and all the positive aspects of running a successful business, it would be remiss of me not to mention these :

Accountants and lawyers are not nearly the best sources of business advice.

Banks may or may not wish to lend you money. Either way I recommend that you avoid them. Starting a business with borrowed money is not my idea of fun.

Credit too should be a no-no. I describe throughout this book how to have your customers finance your business.

Don't fool yourself with concepts and ideas for your business which you haven't properly qualified and backed up by hard facts, real attributes and a detailed explanation of all the steps in the business process and how they will function.

Elevator pitches are as seductive and misleading to yourself as they are to listeners. A short description of your idea, product or company delivered in a way that anyone can quickly understand is often used as a substitute for a real business plan. It's not.

Fatal flaw is to forget, neglect or plain not know to carry out a strategic analysis or external review of the environment in which your business will operate now and in the future. Without this you are just taking a blind leap of faith.

Go big on market research, it's money well spent. New and existing small businesses spend on average less than twenty percent of invested money on marketing. That's too little. Underestimating the importance of marketing is possibly the biggest single blunder you can make when coming into business. You must know about identification, selection and development of your product or service; determination of price; selection of distribution channels to reach the consumer; development and implementation of a promotional strategy and branding. You must spend on these.

Hard to do are trade sales. They may be easy to say but if you don't have direct trade to trade sales experience and contacts within the industry/sector in which you are trading then you will struggle.

Important beyond words are relationships. Building them is a long term strategy but they create trust and trust leads to revenue. A long term and profitable business - isn't that what you want?

Chapter 13

A RECIPE FOR SUCCESS

Whether you are self-employed, an entrepreneur, an internet marketer or running your own business of any kind or even if you are just an 'ordinary Joe' intent on leading a happy life, there's a couple of questions critical to your well-being which you must consider -

* *Do you think that you will perform better or worse at what you do by being self-critical?*

* *Do you think you will perform better or worse by knowing what other like-minded individuals are doing and how they operate?*

* *Do you think you will perform better or worse by engaging with others who have different views and aspirations from your own?*

Okay, that's three questions ... but ... as you no doubt realise, all three are closely connected. Each relates to questioning how you and others are going about your business. The questions highlight the importance of acquiring regular market intelligence, questioning what is going on and why, and developing strategies based on both your own and others' ideas, opinions and practices.

In short you need to constantly self-evaluate and you must communicate with the marketplace, or society at large, in order to prosper. There is no other way to properly maintain the vigour and health of your life or commercial operation.

Some sectors of society do not set a good example in this respect. There are those who show no interest in engaging with anyone expressing different views. They stick to entrenched positions with no evidence base other than the belief that 'they are right'. There is no listening to (let alone understanding of) counter views, no willingness to consider or engage with empirical evidence that challenges their position.

There is an arrogance - the arrogance of ignorance - to this inherent belief that one is so obviously right that no opposition is tolerated. Don't let this be you. Keep an open mind, form your opinions and plan your strategies accordingly. Base your future on well researched and broad based knowledge. Then by all means zero in on a specific approach.

Beware too - the arrogance of intellect. In this state you may be well informed, but you seek out and consider only evidence that supports your point of view and are dismissive of any counter-indications. Be self-confident but never have such belief in the rightness of your views as to leave no room for doubt. Proceed on the basis of self-awareness and justification, rather than assertion. Consider all relevant angles.

This, for good example, is what lawyers do, also academics and politicians worth their salt. They understand that they have a common interest in knowing all sides of an issue. Even when advocating the case for one side, derived from a particular philosophy or brief, they need to be aware of the counter-arguments.

So be it for you. Cultivate understanding of the views and abilities of others and be aware of the limitations of your own position. You can then reflect in order to overcome any weaknesses or adapt your position. Remember that success in business or life generally is dependent on having - *A definitive long term goal* but with *Short term analytics and flexibility*. This approach empowers you, makes you a more formidable adversary. It is a sign of strength.

~

The Scottish tradition of porridge making and eating is awash with folklore, myth and ritual. Custom dictates that the oats and water mix (never milk) must be stirred right-handed and clockwise with a wooden spurtle while cooking. The porridge should then be eaten with a deer horn spoon from a birch wood bowl, while standing, not seated!

Critically, a pinch of salt is added. This last point is quintessentially Scottish. In most other cultures some sweetener, sugar or honey, is added – but that is absolutely taboo to Scots. It is in fact easy to identify real Scots in breakfast bars or other public eateries by the fact that they are the ones vociferously insistent on having a pinch of salt in their porridge!

A common misconception is that the term 'taken with a pinch of salt' - in reference to expressing a degree of scepticism with regard to something stated - derives from the Scots' love of salt in their porridge and to their notoriously canny nature. Not so. The term 'taking it with a pinch of salt' when having reservations about a fact or statement being completely true derives from Roman times when a grain of salt was considered to be an antidote to certain poisons. The more general corollary being that food is more easily ingested if taken with a small amount of salt – and likewise questionable truths!

Whatever the origins of the colloquial expression, there is little doubt that (Scottish porridge eater or otherwise) it's an important idiom to remember in today's era of fake news, biased media, censored internet and untrustworthy politicians. As regards all of these entities it might well be wise to apply a bucket load of salt to their outpourings rather than just a pinch! This is even more relevant to those of you who are entrepreneurs, business owners or self-employed.

The success of your business is, after all, dependent on sound intelligence on which to base decisions. You cannot properly plan your strategies if working according to flawed facts and figures. You must be sure to use reliable sources of information; ones which, as with the Scottish porridge making tradition, have a well established pedigree. You need a system for doing this. Fortunately it's quite easy. Here's how :

Compare recipes - Refer to as many different ways of making porridge as you can find. Immediately discard those which are clearly unsuitable. Prepare the others and find which ones are easiest to cook and which are most agreeable to your palate. With a little trial and error you will establish a reliable favourite, a recipe to successfully produce the finest porridge every time. Apply the same principle with information sources – sift through them, compare and taste. Do not depend on just one source and never until it is proven. And weigh up views from reliable sources on all sides of the spectrum.

Stick to what you know - Once you have that successful recipe, stick to it. It takes time and practice to find just the right ingredients, method of preparation and a flavour that appeals – a porridge which you 'know, like and trust'. Information sources and business associates are the same. Take time to establish your sources and relationships. Weed out those which are disagreeable and then work only with those who have proven their long term reliability.

Trust your gut - If the porridge makes you vomit, don't use that recipe again! But, even before you reach such a critical stage, you should note if the porridge recipe you are using feels right. Is the look and smell of the preparation dubious? Is there anything at all in fact with which you are not at ease? If in any doubt at all discard it. Your gut, as in your stomach, knows best – hence the term 'gut instinct'. This 'sixth sense' regarding people and events in our lives resides in all of us but not everyone heeds its guidance. But those who listen to and 'follow their gut' in all sorts of life and business situations are most often well rewarded. So go with your 'gut feeling' more often. It exists for a reason, trust what it tells you - no pinch of salt required!

Joseph T.Riach

Chapter 14

MY WORD IS MY BOND

My word is my bond is not an expression that you hear much these days. You're even less likely to come across it actually being applied in practice – and that's a shame. Because those words hark back to a time when a person's word was binding. It was considered dishonourable to go back on ones word. Today is different.

Today there is a lack of trust. There is a lack of trust because people lack respect for others, the latter being fundamentally due to their own lack of self respect. After all if you don't trust yourself to behave with decency then you're not going to expect to find it in anyone else. If you want others to behave with honesty and integrity then you must first start to behave with honesty and integrity yourself. You must *lead by example.*

Today everything in business (and life generally too) is contracts and litigation. Selfishness and greed pervades much of society. Rapacious lawyers and government give it momentum. Politicians interfere in ever more areas of people's lives and the legal profession actively promotes the 'blame game' in liability claim litigation. They also encourage ever more complex contractual arrangements and more of them. Yet, as regards contracts, any lawyer will tell you that there isn't a contract which man can write which another man can't break.

POWER POINT - *"There is not a contract man can conceive which another man can't break."*

The more complex the content of a contract then the more scope there is for that content, the wording or the substance, to be challenged. In other words, the more contracts there are and the more complex they are, simply provides more work for the legal profession. Many contracts, and often the legal profession, are of little benefit to the general public.

In practical application a contractual dispute will not be 'won' by the party 'in the right'. It will be won by the party with the most financial muscle, the one who can afford to take it furthest into litigation.

Where's the justice in that? Where is the benefit of such a system to you and I? Would we not be better reverting to a simple handshake and honouring it? Then we'd have no expensive lawyers, no meaningless papers. Most significantly, we'd take responsibility for our own actions and put ourselves back in control of our own destiny.

POWER POINT - *"Take responsibility for your own actions and put yourself in control of your own life."*

Some years ago I drafted a franchise agreement for a project in which I was involved. I was very thorough in my work, covering every conceivable point and including in fine legalese lots of *'in-the-event-ofs'*, *'not-with-standings'* and *'wherein-as-befores'!!*

On completion I took the document along to a local lawyer to have it checked. After a thirty minute examination it was declared perfect, flawless – not a single alteration was recommended. I was then charged several hundred pounds sterling for the consultation! Not surprisingly I quickly resolved to write all of my own contracts from then forward and forego having them scrutinised by a law firm. Subsequently I produced contracts for my clients too and at a fraction of the cost charged by lawyers.

To this day, I will write contracts for clients. Just as often I recommend that they don't use one; that they proceed on trust and a shake of the hand. That they practice the *'My word is my bond'* philosophy.

I give this advice because I myself have not used contracts for my own work for several years ... and, believe me, I get along just fine without them. Critics will not only say that this practice is risky but also that my refusal to do contractual work is typically losing me a substantial percentage of potential clients. My response to this last point is that I'm gaining one hundred per cent of the clients with whom I wish to work! By definition, these are honourable clients who present no risk at all!

POWER POINT - *"Filter out potential clients and time wasters with whom, for whatever reason, you don't want to work. The ones with whom you do want to work will be low risk, low hassle, high profit."*

When you work only with those clients who are agreeable to a non-contractual arrangement you will be employing the *'I Want'* business principle; that's where your business plan is based on your 'wants' – in this case 'I want to work only on a non contractual basis'. Additionally you will be *spending all of your time only with quality clients* rather than wasting the bulk of your time with clients who do not conform to your *'I*

Want' business plan.

Here is a real example of one of my non-contractual business arrangements :

For many years I have run my *Wake Up Leisure and Learning Breaks**. These are residential holiday experiences but with ongoing personal tuition from me throughout. I pass on to my guests my views and experience of building wealth and a successful life or business - **and let them see it at work!** In conducting this business-

- Guests contact me and arrange their visit by email
- There is no exchange of contract
- They say they'll arrive and I say I'll be there for them
- When they arrive they pay me for my services
- When they pay me then I provide my services

That's it, simple. No contracts, no lawyers and no extra cost, just trust. I trust the guest to turn up and to pay me. The guest trusts me to be there and to provide the service.

The only risk to me would be if the guest didn't show. It's never happened and if it did, it wouldn't concern me.

The risk to the guest is if I am not there to meet them, but they haven't yet paid me anything and I do have assistance. So risk negligible, contract unnecessary.

The biggest point is this : *I have deliberately constructed the business this way!*

POWER POINT - *"Construct your business and your life and the manner in which they operate to suit your personal wants."*

The type of the business I've constructed and the quality

of the people who therefore get involved (those to whom their word is their bond and for whom their integrity is their most valued asset) means that the business is sure to succeed on a strictly *'My Word Is My Bond'* basis. It proves conclusively that, if we want it enough we can, even in the modern world, work without contracts and work according to *'My Word Is My Bond.'*

POWER POINT - *"Choose to work only with quality people to whom their word is their bond and for whom their integrity is their most valued asset."*

Foot Note : Even where no written contract has been entered into, a contractual arrangement can still in law be deemed to exist (depends on jurisdiction and circumstance). Litigation can still be pursued where considered necessary but without having incurred the front end fuss of documentation and legal fees.

Wake Up Leisure and Learning Breaks.
Personal Mentoring and Business Guidance in southern Portugal.
https://www.tomriach.com . Click 'Wake Up'.

Joseph T.Riach

Chapter 15

YOUR WORD IS YOUR BRAND

When you practice the principle of 'My Word Is My Bond' you are presenting yourself to the wider world in a very particular way. A way exclusive to you. This is what is known as your **Brand**. You will be recognised by it. You have established what you expect of yourself and thereby what your audience expects. You must now consistently represent your brand in all that you say and do. Every part of your persona and all your presentations in person or in media will portray the same you. The you that is your brand.

You've decided to be self-employed. Great, but what now? There are literally millions of other self-employed people out there competing to have their work recognised. How are you going to stand out among them?

The answer is to understand that you are now the main shareholder of your own little company. You are also the managing director and the sole employee carrying out all the functions within the business. These functions critically include marketing and you are now Head of Marketing for the brand called *'You'!*

As this special brand, you will need to stand out from all other businesses. In order to do that you will have to be clear in your own mind as to the specific benefits which you offer in your chosen field so that you can be sure to connect with the right audience. A good starting point is to ask yourself two questions :

1. **Why would someone employ my business?**
2. **What is it that I'm promising?**

Get the answers to those questions clearly defined within your brand and you'll be well on your way!

But there's lots more to consider .....

Your Niche

You must sift through all the services you intend for your new business to provide. Tick off those which most appeal to you, which you most readily see yourself doing and are likely to have the greatest client appeal. Now you need to narrow it down. The narrower the better. Customers will not turn to your work because you are a specialist in every department; they will come to you because you are a specialist in a specific department!

POWER POINT - *"Customers do not come to you because you are a specialist in every department, they come to you because you are a specialist in a specific department."*

In what area are you a specialist? Identifying the answer to that question will go a long way to establishing what your brand will be and how others will recognise it.

By finding your niche, your area of specialist ability, you will establish not only the basis of your personal brand but also the route to creating income. The public are after all not looking just for good businesses to serve their needs but for ones with particular areas of speciality. When deciding on the specific goods or services you will supply and on how to deliver them it pays to :

- **Rely on experience** – *Use your knowledge of your*

past employment, hobbies, relationships, clubs or school, any subject of which you have experience ... and passion!

- **Be specific** – *Promoting just 'Whisky' for example is too general. 'Scotch Whisky' is better. But 'Single Malt Scotch Whisky' is best. Get it?*

- **Target Lucrative Sectors** – *Promoting medicaments and wellness products and practices could, for example, be of high value. It's a big money sector. You're more likely to earn well there than in the sale of Elizabethan era underwear for example (fascinating as the latter subject undoubtedly is)!*

- **Target a particular audience** – *Should you choose to sell Elizabethan underwear however, then you want your brand to appeal to the appropriate socioeconomic groups. In this instance perhaps historians, clothes designers, students of Elizabethan culture etc. But whatever your subject, knowing who your customers are is essential to help you to customise your approach and your brand.*

- **Study** – *Just like any other subject you will improve your craft and the marketing of your brand by continuous learning and study. Mixing with your peers both online and off will heighten your awareness of what's 'hot' and where there exists market opportunities which you and your brand can exploit. Listening and learning are crucial to success in any venture, don't neglect it here!*

Your Value

For buyers to recognise you and your brand they have to be able to see the value that you undertake to deliver to them through your business. This is done not just by telling them what it is that you do but by explaining how you do it. It is, if you like, a promise of a certain quality. As with all promises, when you come up with the goods then you have won a friend for life. Here's an examples of a brand promise pertaining to another of my books :

Mastering the Art of Making Money : *This book is all about the acquisition of financial and material wealth. It contains a direct account of how the author created a fortune.*

While you want to promote your work to the full within your brand promise, it's best to slightly *understate on a promise* – in that way you can then *over-deliver!* My sincere hope for example, is that this book turns out to be of even greater value to you than you had first expected when purchasing.

YourWhy?

Now ... why do you do what you do? Why are you involving yourself in your particular business? You'd better know because if you don't then you may as well pack it in right now. You see it's all about conviction. Without it you're lost. Your customers will experience no engagement with you. With conviction you are sharing profound emotions with your audience :

- *I can't sleep nights for thinking of ...*
- *I'm angry and I want to change things!*
- *I'm so excited by what's happening at ...*

Get it? Let your customers see the real you. Share your feelings with them. Engage them with your passion.

Here's how I apply the emotion, the driver, the 'Why' to my '*Mastering the Art of Making Money*' book :

"I'm overjoyed that life has given me the opportunity to

share with everyone the means to enjoy the same full and happy life with which I've been blessed."

So be true to your convictions. Work with the power and emotion driven by them and you will find that your brand and your promise become widely recognised and sought after. When that happens you will truly have arrived as a self-employed business trader of merit.

~

There are many variations to the formula for branding yourself in business. Your approach will be largely dependent on the line of work in which you are involved.

The British music hall entertainer and actor Max Wall, would often attribute his success to 'a song, a dance and a silly walk' – these being the basic elements which he deemed it necessary to include in his performance in order to captivate his audience. He became identified with them – they were his brand.

While I do not advocate adopting that approach in the boardroom, not literally anyway, figuratively speaking it's not a bad mental attitude to employ. After all if you are upbeat, humorous and 'whistling a happy tune' (inside your head at least) what better way could there be to approach your work?

Wall also possessed a natural tragicomic facial expression of the kind associated with the classic clown face. He used this to great effect in enacting the pathos inherent in his stage performances; as well as it being a great asset in the many straight acting roles of his later career. In fact, such was his prowess as a serious actor that it was once said of him that he made Laurence Olivier look like an amateur!

As regards business, I've long felt that acting is a skill which can be highly valuable in the commercial world. I learned early on, for instance, that the first solicitor to represent me in my various business and personal affairs was a skilled, stone wall actor. In consultations he adopted a dead pan expression and a steady stare which never wavered throughout the meeting. Therefore he was impossible to read. You couldn't know his thoughts. It was an impressive performance.

Then there are politicians. Are they not to a man, and woman, quintessentially actors? The 'best' of them can portray a different character to suit any occasion, a face for every situation and a pose to befit any circumstance. Their public face is often the epitome of fine acting as they deny the undeniable, defend the indefensible and turn every question asked of them into an opportunity to deliver their well rehearsed lines. Yes, they are actors.

In order to succeed in business, there is therefore a strong line of argument which suggests that the ability to act is a useful talent to possess. If you don't possess it, then perhaps you should seek to learn the skill. It could stand you in good stead in all sorts of face-to-face situations.

The key point though is, rather than working to develop the ability to effectively pretend that you're someone other than yourself – someone more polished, stronger, more worldly, more sophisticated, whatever - why not devote that same energy to learning to perform better as yourself? For, regardless of what you might gain by playing out a part which is not you, just think of the gain to be had in being a better version of yourself. That is what you should aspire to.

POWER POINT - *"Perform – but perform as a better version of yourself."*

Identify your own strengths then work at the way you present yourself and them to the world. This will become your identity, your brand. Many entrepreneurs fail to do this. They have the ability, the knowledge, the wherewithal to do great things in the market place but fail to deliver it in such a way as to win the business.

As Oscar Schindler, the master salesman in the classic film Schindler's List, replies when asked what his role in the business will be, he responds, accompanied by an expansive hand gesture - "Presentation!" Yes, presentation is everything.

POWER POINT - *"Presentation is everything!"*

As was the case with myself in my early years in business, I concentrated on the quality of my service and did indeed deliver excellence. Yet I failed to prosper because I didn't understand the importance of presentation – of presenting myself, of acting out my brand. Once I developed my personality, worked on my presentation skills and promoted myself with verve and charisma, I never looked back.

So think presentation, create a memorable persona for your audience and act out the best version of yourself. Present your very own song, dance and silly walk!

~

There was a time when most budding entrepreneurs first acquired premises, a shop or office, put up their shiny new sign with their name on it above the door, sat back in their new and expensive leather recliner and waited for the business to roll in. And waited … and waited …

No customers arrived of course, other than a handful of tyre kickers and inquisitive non-buyers. What did besiege them, and in droves, were advertising sales people representing every journal, magazine, billboard, radio and television network company in the land. Each one 'guaranteeing' bigger audiences and more and more assured clients and sales. The embattled business owner paid out ever bigger advertising fees to all and sundry ... and waited for the business to roll in ... and waited.

But, while most budding entrepreneurs acted in this way, a few didn't. A few, just a few, didn't invest in showy premises, costly advertising or even a fancy leather chair. In fact they spent little to no money at all other than on inexpensive business cards and simple flyers. They chose instead to 'get on their bike' (some literally) and visit every single person or business who, by dint of their trade, profession or known preferences, identified as a likely buyer. They met their prospective clients face to face and - horror of horrors - spoke to them! These enterprising few were the ones who prospered.

POWER POINT - *"Successful entrepreneurs 'get on their bike' and speak to prospects and clients face to face."*

In today's internet world much has changed – or has it?

Many budding internet marketers set up a website, create shiny advertising banners with their offer on them, post them all over the internet and .... sit back in their new and expensive leather recliners and wait for the business to roll in. They wait ... and wait ... Still no customers arrive, other than a handful of tyre kickers and inquisitive non-buyers. Sound familiar?

Then, just like their real world and bricks and mortar business colleagues before mentioned, they find themselves besieged, not by buyers, but by web site owners, agents, advertising sales people, affiliate marketers and 'gurus', each claiming to be the sole source of the holy grail which will direct real buyers to them in their tens of millions. The embattled business owner pays out for the latest hardware, software programme or training course 'guaranteed' to produce customers, puts the plan into action and waits for the business to roll in ... and waits.

Yet, for the thousands, nay millions, who behave and wait in this way, a few, just a few don't. Yes, they post their banner ads and spread their word on the internet but they target their promotions to just those niche markets and the people within them who are most likely to want the product or service on offer. This takes market research and work – yes work!

When they have stimulated the interest of the right people, they don't sit around in fancy leather chairs, or any chair for that matter, they 'get on their bikes' (some literally), or at least get on the phone to speak personally to every single person or business who, by dint of their initial response, trade, profession or known preferences, have identified themselves as likely buyers. Yes – they speak to their prospects!

Guess what? These enterprising few are the ones who prosper.

POWER POINT - *"Do your market research and target your promotional work to the niche where your buyers are."*

To this day, I speak to clients. Apart from the sheer pleasure of interacting with them directly, they can in this way inform me more accurately of just what it is that they are looking for and I can communicate more clearly how I can assist them to reach their goals. Everyone wins. One client or customer who knows, likes and trusts you through such personal contact is worth a thousand tyre kickers who don't! It is a simple sense approach which reduces time, stress and cost while increasing effectiveness, satisfaction and profit.

What business person in their right mind would not choose to proceed in a way which creates more profit for less and more pleasurable work?

Note that work is involved. That's another key. The internet particularly, and more so than even a lazy budding business person lolling in his recliner waiting for business to magically arrive, gives newcomers to self-employment the false impression that finding success is 'easy'. If only! There's work involved ... and lots of it.Those who succeed put in the hours, the hard graft, the learning and the education, and then they apply it rigorously day after day, year after year, non stop.

POWER POINT - *"Never think that success comes work free. Waiting for success is a long wait."*

They become specialists in their field, masters of their craft. They realise that their success or failure directly reflects their skill in relating to, and engaging with, their clients and customers. This attitude is the exact opposite of what those affected by the shiny shop sign syndrome display. If waiting for business to come to you, then you are in for a long wait.

That's not to say that opportunities do not abound. They are everywhere, all around. But they won't fall into the lap of those sitting around doing nothing to attract them. You have to be out there in the business arena working, planning and scheming before the opportunities present themselves. It is only by being involved that you learn to spot opportunities.

There are darned few shortcuts to success in business but developing your ability to identify opportunities and to act on them decisively is one. If you are always putting yourself out there, are always alert to a possible opening, always focussed on your goal, always performing to the best of your ability, then the openings will come.

There is no one sure route to success. No single rule to follow. Success comes to the few who find it mainly from bloody minded determination and opportunity grabbing. You never know where your break will come from so you have to be on high alert for it all the time. It won't arrive like a bolt of lightening. Big breaks are rare. Much more common is a series of small breaks, each one a step on the stairway to success.

~

There was a time when pubs sold beer and spirits and little else. Folks went there to enjoy a drink. If you wanted something to snickle on then a bag of potato crisps or maybe peanuts was the most you were likely to get.

Then one pub owner, Sandy McKay, had the bright idea to sell food. He settled on one simple wholesome snack, a hot minced beef pie and chips, which would go down well before, during or after a belly full of beer. The punters flocked in!

At a landlords' association meeting a couple of months after launching his hot food strategy, Sandy was quizzed about his new initiative.

"Do you sell a lot of pies and chips?"

"Oh yes."

"But do you make any money from it?"

"No, nothing at all."

"Then why do you do it?"

"Ah – you should see all the beer that I sell!"

Sandy, you see, was more than just a pub landlord or even a businessman. He was an entrepreneur. He was prepared to innovate and take risks. And he (perhaps unwittingly) demonstrated three key elements in entrepreneurial behaviour -

* Inventiveness – He looked for and created solutions as to how to increase trade

* Loss Leader – He was prepared to sell something at a loss in order to make a profit on his main line

* Incentive – He understood that he had to give his customers an added incentive to come to his pub

- and in doing this he prospered.

Soon afterwards, another pub in town started giving away free fish and chip suppers for one hour each Friday evening. The proprietor reported selling more drink in that one evening than in all the other nights of the week put together!

Eventually it became the normal thing for all pubs to sell food. In many cases the catering side of the business overtook the drinks side both in terms of revenue and in being the main activity of the enterprise. So the beer, spirits and wines were the added incentive for people to come and eat there!

There was another interesting development. A couple of landlords realised that there was a market niche of drinkers who did not want to go to a pub which had effectively become a restaurant rather than a traditional watering hole. They made a point of not providing food. They advertised their pubs as being purely drinking establishments. The drinkers rolled in!

These pub owners were therefore capitalising on providing a service to a niche market of patrons who wished solely to drink and specifically not be in a place serving food or surrounded by people eating. These owners too were displaying -

* Creativity

* Niche Recognition

and

* Branding and Marketing Ability

They were prepared to try different strategies in order to keep pace with, or get ahead of, market trends. Better still, those like Sandy McKay, were actually creating the market trends!

POWER POINT - *"Inventive entrepreneurs create market trends."*

~

Mr.Carpenter employed a different approach. He was Carpenter by name and a carpenter to trade. His workshop was crammed full of coffins in various stages of preparation, all on order to the undertaker whose funeral parlour was located next door. When the undertaker passed away (yes they pop their clogs too), Mr.Carpenter bought that business.

He also acquired the disused country manor at the end of the same street and opened it as a retirement home. For good measure he purchased for Mrs.Carpenter two nearby shop units which were converted for use as a creche and children's preschool nursery.

All the while Mr.Carpenter continued with his local authority contract work in the renovation of old town properties into modern apartments for let to newly weds.

Carpenter rarely felt the need to advertise his businesses, any of them. Clientele passed from one enterprise to the next in a continuous flow as the various stages of their lives unfolded. Plus there were referrals.

Mr.Carpenter had constructed the perfect business model. A veritable cradle to grave solution. One with multiple income streams and a guaranteed customer base.

Many hugely successful entrepreneurs operate in a similar manner. They build up a series of 'crossover businesses'; enterprises which are inter-related, continuous and feed each other with repeat business and sales.

I developed my own business in just such a way. But, in the first instance, I became an entrepreneur unwittingly .....

~

My grandfather was a master baker in the city of his birth which was, at the time, the largest fishing port in Europe. As such my earliest work experience, early morning, after school and weekend jobs were in his bakery and in the fishing industry.

The bakery was hot, an open-necked, sleeves rolled up environment where I learned to knead dough with easy-going, flour-ghosted tradesmen, bake bread and gorge myself on scorching hot Scotch pies straight from the oven! I needed them. Because from the bakery I high-tailed it on foot most mornings to the fish docks, freezing cold in the early hours of winter days, to unload trawlers, pack their cargo of wet fish in ice and deliver the bulky boxes to the fish processing houses for gutting and filleting.

Where the atmosphere in the bakery was chirpy and cheerful, busy but sometimes subdued, the fish industry was an ever loud, vulgar, rough-and-tumble world, peopled by tough trawlermen and even tougher fishwives! The bakery taught me the skill of baking and the language of rolls, 'softies', loaves and 'fancies'. At the docks I learned how to handle, grade and cut fish and the coarse talk of the hardened souls which went with it.

I also learned, not surprisingly, that fishworkers bought bread from the bakery and that bakers purchased fish from the fishmonger. On this realisation was my first enterprise born. It was a barter style arrangement whereby I supplied my friends at the docks with morning rolls and bakery goods and my baker colleagues with fresh fish.

Each day the dockworkers awaited my arrival from the bakery before enjoying their early morning tea break with the hot rolls and pies I brought them. The bakers in turn relished my return from the docks with my fishy cargo before knocking off for the day and taking their fresh cod, haddock or herring home to their families for lunch.

I now had three jobs, a foot in two industries, friends from many different backgrounds and the education and future contacts to go with them. Of course I was neither the maker of the bread nor the catcher of the fish, the prime wealth creation activities, but, as a middleman between the two, I had unwittingly become a young entrepreneur! Later in life I would create my own goods and services but for now I was earning in both real terms and, more importantly as I would discover, in experience and goodwill.

In due course my grandfather retired and the fish industry died. But the need of the populace to be fed lives on. There is always a market for fresh food.

And there's always a market for entrepreneurs and innovators willing to use their native wit, get their hands dirty and grind that bit harder than the rest – for those working on excellence.

Grandad, the bakers and the fish workers all knew that. I know it too. So should you.

Chapter 16

WORKING ON EXCELLENCE

Most people yearn for success of one kind or another. Accruing financial wealth is what is in mind with many in that respect but success can, of course, apply to many areas of life and can arrive in many forms. Regardless though of what your perception of success may be, there is one over-riding determination which applies to all endeavours - and that is,

"How motivated are you in your pursuit of success?"

A lot of words are written and spoken about motivation. It can be different things to different people, motivation comes in many guises. Yet I feel that all motivation can be boiled down to, and summed up in, one simple question -

"How bad do you want it?"

Put it this way : Imagine I were to ask you,

"What is the longest distance you could possibly run without stopping, the absolute maximum you could manage before collapsing exhausted?"

You give me your answer, to which I then say,

"Okay. Could you run one mile further than that if I were to give you one million dollars?" Then again I add,

"And what about if I ran behind you holding a loaded gun to your head which I will fire at you if you stop?"

You see, it's easy to say that you want something real bad

when you're shooting the breeze with friends, lounging at home or passing time in the pub; but when the going gets tough, do you really want that something crushingly bad enough?

You'll often feel in life that you have nothing more to give, that you've reached your limit and can carry on no further. Yet you have hidden reserves and strength in you (we all do) which just demands the right circumstance in order for you to find it. That circumstance can be activated in several ways, but mostly through reward and even more so through fear.

Great achievers though do not wait for such prompts, they activate the power voluntarily. They search for and find that burning desire within themselves and plumb the depths of their very soul to bring that resolve to the surface. Then they apply it relentlessly with the same determination as the guy running for the million dollars or the one running for his life. Such titans will tell you that the best moments in their lives occur when, faced with seemingly impossible impediments, they reach down and find inner strength where they thought none existed.

Can you find such motivation within you? Success - How bad do you want it?

~

Knowing that I had given up competitive sport many years previously, my near neighbour asked me,

"Why then did I continue to run full blast each day up and down the mountain track behind our homes?"

My answer was crisp and clear.

"Two reasons. Secondly, if I don't run up it today, I won't

be able to run up it tomorrow." I paused to let that sink in.

"So it's kind of self-regenerating then?" he eventually queried, then continued, "What's the first reason?"

"The first reason," I shot back confidently, "Is that today is the only day that I have to do it."

"What about tomorrow?" he immediately countered with a sly grin.

"Tomorrow," I said, "Will be today when it comes. But for now I only have today, so I must give it my best shot. That's what it's all about you know, giving it your best shot. Whatever your endeavour, pursuit or goal in life, there's little point pursuing it unless you give it all you've got. Also, it's destructive to delay. You must do it now. Then, when the day ends, you know you've been the best you could be. I call it 'Working on Excellence.' "

I had my friend's attention. So I carried on.

"Most of you want to be yourselves. You want to be liked too. You want to be the guy who is always there for others, always approachable and willing to lend a helping hand. You want to be these things but it is by no means easy. Being yourself, attending to your own needs while catering for others at the same time, is often contradictory. Like so many aspects of life it has to be worked at.

Whenever you embark on an exceptional endeavour or mindfully set out to achieve a goal beyond what you have previously reached, you are 'working on excellence'. The question is - can you satisfy your own aspirations for yourself while also sharing your experience and assisting others to seek excellence too?

The answer is 'Yes'. In fact the two go hand in hand.

While you can manage to do both, don't expect to be perfect however. Work according to your physical and mental state, get used to your own capabilities and let your beneficiaries take what they get. No more, no less. Let them catch a ride on your shirt tail on the understanding that they are contributing to your effort by being there. This is key - your action must not be entirely altruistic, there must be something in it for you too. The incoming support and gratefulness must balance your expended time and energy.

While it is hard to measure the costs and returns in relationships, know that giving life energy to others is also a form of receiving energy. It is give and take within a cycle of 'working on excellence'. When you give in this way, expect a return in the form of inspiration, motivation and perspective.

The last mentioned – perspective - can be both humbling and inspiring. Realising that your struggles on the trail of life are insignificant in the big picture is an essential start point to 'working on excellence.'

My slog up the mountain track each day is in pursuit of excellence. I'll never catch it of course but I'll give it a good shot. In the process I'll hopefully inspire and motivate others to give of their best right now, today. Then on tomorrow's today to do the same again."

My friend was quiet for some time. He thought long and hard. When he broke his silence it was to say,

"Can I hitch a ride on your shirt tail and run up the mountain with you tomorrow?"

"No," I replied, "Make it today!"

~

The term 'out of the blue' refers to an event that occurs unexpectedly, without any warning or preparation. It originates from the phenomenon of a sudden thunderstorm striking from an immediately prior clear sky. It is likely that at some point in life you have experienced just such a soaking, most people have! There's a good chance too that you have been subject to some sort of other completely unforeseen circumstance occurring in your life - several probably. As much as an out of the blue experience is unexpected, you can be pretty sure that somewhere, sometime you will be party to one. In other words, you should expect the unexpected!

Yes, the unexpected will find you .. but, and here's the key point .. it won't find you unless you make yourself available. That means putting yourself in the right place so that when the surprise arrives you will be open to receiving it.

If, for example, you never go outside on a sunny day then there is no likelihood of you being caught in an out of the blue downpour. Nor will you get mugged in a dark alley late at night if you never go to such a place at such a time. On the brighter side, what chance is there of you enjoying pleasant surprises if you do not position yourself to receive them?

From an entrepreneurial viewpoint there is only one way to ensure that you are best positioned to benefit from positive windfalls. That is to be self-employed. In that state it is you, rather than someone else, who can take advantage of extraordinary commercial opportunities as they arise.

First of all though, you must work diligently at your chosen enterprise. Work hard, work smart, do all the right things to create a thriving, profitable and fun business. Yes, be sure to enjoy yourself! As you do that, keep an eye out for the unusual, opportunities that may not be directly related to your activity or which may diverge from your chosen direction, but which nevertheless conform to your overall strategy. These 'out of the blues' remember, will not present themselves unless you are already establishing a formidable business presence; that is, you have made yourself available.

Then, some day, the extra big break will just 'drop into your pocket' as if from nowhere. Believe me, it happens. I myself have experienced the phenomenon several times. Some of my most lucrative pieces of work arrived from 'nowhere'. Not all related directly to my mainline work - but I said 'Yes' anyway - and was able to carry out the work because I was in the right place (self-employed and working hard) to receive the surprises when they arrived. This is crucial.

I repeat - it is first essential to be successfully self-employed in the first instance. Make yourself well known, establish your reputation. That is the circumstance in which the windfall business deals may appear as if from nowhere. That is when you will enjoy success - out of the blue!

~

Legendary Scottish comedian, Chic Murray, told the gag of being on a bus which ran out of control down a steep hill and crashed into a wall at the bottom. In the aftermath of the impact he turned to a dazed passenger beside him and punched him on the nose. "Why did you do that?" asked another bewildered traveller. "Too good a chance to miss!" cracked Chic.

A cruel bit of fun perhaps but Chic's point is well made.

You must be ready to take advantage of opportunities in life whenever and wherever they arise. How do you position yourself to receive them?

There are two things you can do right now.

The first is to get out in your street, your neighbourhood, your town and, without any political objective (that is essential), set about helping others in whatever ways you can.

Become known as an enthusiastic, energetic, concerned and caring individual. Encourage good humour, optimism and personal responsibility. Now you are well known, liked and respected within the community. You gain a reputation built on trust and respect.

The second move is – become self-employed!

Put yourself in the position of being in sole control of your life and the prosperity in it. Learn what it is to be your own man/woman. From that perspective you will see how energising it is to be independent and creating your own destiny. As a self-employee you will understand more clearly the needs of both yourself and your fellow man. Your self-esteem will soar, your motivation too. You will appreciate the responsibilities which come with self-employment but also be able to capitalise on the freedom of your new situation.

One other point – When you set up your enterprise, establish a 'real world' one, a bricks and mortar business. That is not to say you should ignore the internet or modern technology. But many people flooding to work online involve themselves in what are nothing more than pyramid schemes and money cyclers. These neither create wealth nor promote real goods or services. There is no future in them. Use the internet, automated intelligence particularly, by all means, but as the servant and tools of your enterprise.

Then you can build a business of genuine value to your clients, customers and the community at large. One which does not only capitalise on 'bus crash' scenarios but rather which thrives on its own merits, with a reputation for providing ethical value and encouraging freedom of thought and spirit. Put simply, make what you offer ... too good a chance to miss!

~

As regards opportunity .....

Michael Caine, the film star, tells the story of being seated in his own restaurant in London one evening when he was approached by a slightly tipsy diner on his way to the men's room.

"I thought this place was supposed to be full of famous movie people?" challenged the man.

"Well, what am I then?" replied Michael in typical good humour.

"You're the owner," said the man, "You don't count."

"Okay," said Michael, "Then who is that sitting at the corner table?"

The man turned and stared long and hard at the gent referred to by Michael. Eventually he said, "I don't know."

Michael replied, "That's Tom Cruise," and continued, "Who is is that standing at the bar?"

Again the man took a long and earnest look at the figure pointed out. Eventually he repeated the same answer, "I don't know."

Michael enlightened him with, "That's Clint Eastwood."

At that the man just shrugged his shoulders and tottered on to his date with nature in the gents'.

A short time later the diner, on his way back from the men's room, again passed Michael seated at his table. This time he didn't stop but simply called over,

"And there's no-one famous in the toilets either!"

The moral of this fun story is two fold.

People only see what they want to see and frequently fail to see opportunities plainly presented to them. Michael Caine, on the other hand, is famous for inevitably recognising opportunities and saying 'yes' to everything. As a result he has worked in his chosen profession of movie acting, a notoriously insecure one, nonstop throughout the years.

He is also known as being a joy to work with and a stickler for detail. He prepares for all of his roles, large or small, meticulously and diligently.

As an entrepreneur or self-employed business person you should do the same. Be alert and on the watch for opportunities at all times. The best way to do this is to have a reputation for reliability and quality of performance, just as Michael Caine does. Know yourself, your business, your industry and the people in and around it inside out. Then the opportunities will come your way.

Also be excellent at what you do. Areas to give absolute priority to are -

Sales - This is what brings in the money. Do your selling yourself. You're the best person for it.

Finance - Keep tight control of your money. Personally manage it. Never let anyone else have access to your cash.

Personnel - Delegate and employ by all means but use only people you trust implicitly. Better to employ no-one at all rather than someone you don't trust.

Adherence to these three points is critical to your success. Believe me, I've been there.

I've also been to Michael Caine's restaurant. He wasn't there when I visited but Tom Cruise and Clint Eastwood were. They didn't recognise me.

Had they been there I'd have been sure to grab the opportunity to ask for their autographs. The key is to seize the opportunity and ask for what you want. Ask for the business .....

~

As a youngster I went to the Scottish country dance lessons which my mother ran in a local church hall. There I learned to twirl my way through the 'Dashing White Sergeant', 'Strip The Willow', 'Eightsome Reel' and countless other highland classics.

In later teens I attended Madame Murray's ballroom dancing classes. These took place at six o'clock on a Saturday evening. The tuition was usually followed by a visit to the pub for some 'Dutch courage' in the form of several beers before going on to a local dance hall to 'chat up the birds' and put into practice Madame Murray's teachings. These teachings included all the waltzes, the fox trot, sambas and tango. She even taught jive and rock 'n roll. Not unnaturally, these were my favourites!

An amusing part of her lessons was the assignation of partners for the lessons at the start of each session. Pupils were not allowed to choose a partner. The girls lined up at one side of the hall, the boys on the other. At her command, delivered by microphone from her all-seeing position on the stage at one end of the hall, both lines advanced towards each other.

The idea was that your partner for the evening was whoever you ended up facing as the lines met. But, as the lines converged and it became apparent who your partner might be, shoving and pushing developed in the respective lines as boys and girls jostled to avoid an unwanted partner or to be opposite a preferred one! The operation generally degenerated into a mass brawl with Madame frantically blowing on the whistle she kept for just such indiscipline to try and restore order!

Later, in the dance hall, choosing a partner was more civilised. The lad approached a girl he fancied and, in my north-east corner of Scotland, asked,

"Yi duncin'?" (Are you dancing)?

To which the girl would reply,

"Yi askin'?"

He'd then say,

"I'm askin'."

She, if agreeing, then replied,

"I'm duncin'!"

At which the lad would saunter in a proprietorial manner on to the dance floor with the girl in tow behind.

When the girl declined the invitation to dance, her response was, "Nae chunce!" accompanied by crossing her arms, half turning to her friends and sniggering snarkily with them. The poor reject, ego dented, shuffled off to try elsewhere – or not.

Having suffered my share of such rebuffals, I learned that the best tactic when picking a girl was to avoid asking the stand out beauties, those dazzlers whom most lads were hopelessly attracted to and buzzed around like demented bees. Rather than involve myself as a consumer in what I saw as a 'limited supply and over demand' situation, I targeted my advances at the vast bulk of pretty girls waiting hopefully in the shadows. With little competition, I successfully danced with, and then dated, a stream of extremely agreeable young ladies.

When questioned by my friends as to my regular 'conquests', I advised three things :

1. Become the supply in a market in which there is huge demand rather than the other way around.

2. Provide best in class, well prepared goods or services – in the case of the dance hall, that was me!

3. Ask for the business.

As regards the last point, I never asked, "Yi duncin'?", I asked,

"Do you like the old or the new dance steps?"

This prompted a reply like,

"What's the difference?"

To which I'd take the girl's hand and say,

"C'm on I'll show you!"

Does this approach sound familiar to you? If you're in business it should. Because successful entrepreneurs seek out sectors in which there is huge demand but very little supply. Then, like me, they set about creating the supply and ensuring the provision of best in class goods or services.

Always ask for what you want. If you don't ask you'll remain forever the wallflower in the dance hall. But, when you do ask, and *frame your request compellingly*, then you'll waltz off into the sunset with the belle of the ball. Are you dancing?

Joseph T.Riach

BOOK 3

REWARD!

How To Be A Self-Employed Super Star

Joseph T.Riach

Chapter 17

THE SIMPLE MILLIONAIRE

The tractors, trailers, ploughs, bailing machines, spreaders, sprayers, rakes and multifarious agricultural machinery and equipment were neatly assembled in rows in the field below me. A roup! I pulled over and got out of my car so as to get a better look at the items which would be up for grabs in the auction farm sale (roup) which the poster nailed to the gate announced as taking place the next day. Two immaculate John Deere combine harvesters, almost new and gleaming in their distinctive green livery with prancing stag logo, immediately caught my attention. I knew just who would be interested in those. I jumped back into my car and headed straight for Harry Barclay's house.

Harry was a country lad. With little education he left school at fourteen and followed the family's Scottish farming tradition. He grew his business until he owned farmland all over Britain and more than sixty substantial companies. He was a millionaire many times over.

I had met Harry after buying a house in the same country town where he lived. He took something of a shine to me as a young hopeful making my way in business. In due course, as with all his close friends, I was allowed to walk in unannounced to his home and to his kitchen - Harry ran his entire business empire from there. So when I arrived at his house I did just that.

Harry, in open-necked shirt as always, was seated at the kitchen table when I entered, head down studying papers and telephone to hand. He neither looked up nor said anything. I boiled the kettle, made us each a mug of tea, took them over to the table and sat down. Without ceremony I said,

"There's two brand new combines for sale at the farm down the road. Thought you might be interested."

Without breaking from his work or looking up, he quickly shot back,

"Sold them yesterday!"

With that he went back to his cup of tea and on to his next telephone call. Matter dealt with. Concluded. And it was. Quick and simple.

Since then and throughout my life I have endeavoured to model what I am and my way of working on Harry. I have concentrated on developing an attitude of mind which cuts out all the peripheral 'bull' and sticks to the simple issues. Why? I'll tell you why. Let's look at what happened in the scenario I've just recounted.

The first thing to note is that Harry already knew all about the roup and the particulars of it. Of course he did, he was the master of his industry. It was his business to know everybody in it and to know everything that was going on. How foolish of me as a wet behind the ears greenhorn not to realise that!

The second thing to note is what Harry said; he said, "*Sold* them yesterday." He didn't say, "*Bought* them." He said, "*Sold* them." The reason for my emphasis of what he said and my repetition is that this is one of the two most critical lessons to success in business that I ever learned (the other was to use the power of my subconscious). It is therefore the most valuable piece of learning for you also. Here it is –

Successful entrepreneurs never buy then sell, they first sell and then buy!

The simple sense of the sell then buy philosophy is so powerful that it totally goes over the head of the majority of the populace. If presented to them most will question how it can be. Surely you must buy something before you can sell it? Not so.

Harry's 'sold them yesterday' response told me that his wide knowledge of the industry, what was going on and the people within it, meant that he always knew who was in the market and for what. Long before this roup came around, he knew –

All the machinery and equipment which would be on sale

and

Buyers who were looking for them

Harry contacted those buyers and sold them the combine harvesters. Then he contacted the auction company and agreed the purchase. The machines would not come up for sale on the day of the roup, they'd be passed by as 'withdrawn from sale'.

Harry had taught me the priceless lesson that, to succeed in business, you must first sell before you buy. In that way you need never make a loss. Nor will you ever have cash tied up holding stock; nor ever need financing. Simple and brilliant! So simple in fact that the majority of people cannot see or will not believe that such a practice lies at the very heart of the success and huge wealth of those such as Harry.

Harry also sold only at top dollar and bought only at bottom dollar. His purchases came exclusively from roups, bankrupt and distressed sales. The many farms, prime farmland and stock he owned all over Britain, he only ever bought from the banks who had repossessed them. They came to him at 'debt only' cost.

POWER POINT - *"Buy only at absolute rock bottom dollar."*

Modern society promotes in people the tendency to act in haste and to act based on emotion. This is most clearly evident in buying and selling situations. What I call the *'must-have-it-now'* and the *'act-only-in-crisis'* syndromes. These two traits go a long way to explaining why the majority of people never get to be wealthy. They are squanderers. They squander time, relationships and opportunities just as recklessly as they waste money.

Smart operators like Harry, on the other hand, are predatory opportunists. They do not become so by accident. They employ wit and wiles beyond the scope of most others. Buying is only done with cash in hand, never in a rush and only in *'fire sale'* situations from *'act-only-in-crisis'* sellers.

When they sell, they sell to the *'must-have-it-now'* mob, never in a hurry and always at top dollar. Most importantly they **sell before they buy.** They don't shell out their own cash. They use the sale of the goods or services to finance the purchase. The profits they accrue affords them quality time to spend on fostering relationships and waiting for further opportunities. They know that sooner or later the right opportunity will present itself. It always does.

These entrepreneurial Harry types are both patient and smart. Not only do they capitalise on the emotion-based and act-in-haste tendencies of the 'must-have-it-now' and the 'act-only-in-crisis' mentality of squanderers, they cleverly choose to deal only in items both necessary and of quality. That way they know that there will always be a ready market.

They also elect to involve themselves in a trade, profession or sector which gives them pleasure. A niche for which they have a real passion. This keeps them sharp in addition to providing a dependable source of income.

The key elements for you to take from their example are -

Realise that labour, manual or mental, will never make you wealthy

Trading, buying and selling goods or services, is the smart way to prosper

Trade in something which excites you, which brings daily joy into your life

Never sell out of desperation nor buy on emotion.

When you are ready to act in these ways, then you are ready to become part of 'The Secret World Of Self-Employment' - like Harry Barclay.

Harry's success made him both popular and unpopular in equal measure. Many in the farming community saw him as a vulture feeding of the carrion of other farmers' failures. Others saw in him a guardian angel; one who rescued farms, and often whole communities, from ruthless developers and asset strippers. And he was indeed a generous man.

Although he would not help out a failing business (he'd

wait until it went bust), he would give assistance to those ousted from their farms and often re-employed them as operations managers. As such they retained the roof over their heads, management of the practical aspects of their farm and enjoyed a regular wage. They only lost financial control. Harry and his specialist team assumed management and responsibility for the commercial aspects of the business. A win-win situation.

POWER POINT - *"Be ruthless in business but generous in life."*

~

Harry, of course, had no option but to become a farmer. It was a generational family business which he was brought up to. For you today, deciding to become your own boss is a career/lifestyle choice. No-one forces it on you. As I have previously stated, when I decided to become self-employed and set up my own business, I did not ask anyone's permission to do so. Why would I? I knew that I had to accept responsibility for my own actions, my success or my failure. Such self belief lies at the heart of an entrepreneur.

I trust myself to behave responsibly. I start by doing those things necessary to survive, then I do what's possible to further my cause. Then, almost magically, I find myself achieving the impossible.

I spend only what I can afford and anything I don't have the money for, I do without or until I have created the wealth to support it. I am highly competitive and often ruthless in pursuing my goals. Yet I am not indifferent to the needs of others. At the heart of most entrepreneurs there beats a generous pulse. There is a simple explanation for this apparent contradiction.

The fact is that, however determined and committed to success I am, my very adventurism inevitably means that I encounter difficulties and failed efforts along the way. At moments of hardship I have found myself brought back from the edge, revived and restored by improbable allies - friends and colleagues oft neglected, angels of mercy, mysterious strangers and the simple hand of friendship proffered by well-wishers.

It is perfectly consistent therefore that I, and those like me, empathise with those we encounter who are struggling to get by. My generosity though is not blind, it is selective.

Other than donating material relief in desperate situations, I'm inclined to help only those prepared to help themselves. A case of like helping like so that all can thrive. The *'help others to help themselves to help you'* philosophy is central to how successful entrepreneurs work on a daily basis. It underpins how society prospers. It lies at the heart of an entrepreneur.

~

A destitute stranger came to my door. He asked for money. I gave him none but took him in out of the cold and fed him hot food and drink. I found a warm jacket for him and I sent him on his way with a copy of my *'Mastering The Art Of Making Money'* book. I suggested that he read it..

The following day, the same fellow returned to my house. This time he brought with him a wife and three children. Again he asked for money and clearly expected me to help him as previously. So I did. I gave him no money but took food and drinks out on a tray to them and some clothes and toys for the children too. I sent them on their way with a copy of my *'Self-Improvement Should Be Fun!'* book and suggested that they read it..

On the third day the vagrant appeared again. This time with an expanded family of twelve adults and children. They asked for money and were somewhat aggressive in insisting that I help them. I gave them no money but did feed them soup and sandwiches in the driveway. They eventually left, albeit reluctantly, and I gave them a copy of my *'Winning Big In Life And Business'* book which I suggested they should read.

The day after that, I was disturbed from my work by a commotion outside my house. When I went to investigate I found a crowd of fifty or more ruffians, led by the recipient of my goodwill of the previous days, jostling on the sidewalk outside my home They were shouting threateningly and waving placards bearing insults and demands that I give them money, shelter and food. I called the police..

After the police had arrived, dispersed the rioters and taken the ringleader into custody, I went outside to clear up the litter left behind by the mob. Among the general debris of cigarette butts, booze bottles and human waste, I found … the tattered remains of my three books..

In reflecting on events later, I concluded that - "If you give a man a fish he will eat for one day. If you teach a man to fish he will eat every day. But – a man who has no interest in, and no intention of, learning to fish will return for free fish every day until there are no fish left and the pond is destroyed."

Some months after these events, while engaged in writing *'Too Early For A Glass Of Wine?'* there came a knock at my door. I thought not to answer but, after some hesitation, relented and went to see who was there. When I opened the door, there stood a scraggy young waif. He was clearly penniless and looked in need of a good meal. But, when he spoke, he requested neither money nor food. What he did ask for both pleased and surprised me.

"Can I read your books sir?" he pleaded, "I want to make something of my life." .

I held the door open and invited him in.

Joseph T.Riach

Chapter 18

CREATIVE SOLUTIONS

Throughout my business life I have worked as a Creative Solutions Specialist – or in popular parlance – a trouble-shooter. In that role I have assisted major corporations, companies, small businesses and self-employed individuals to devise and implement strategic change and to resolve troublesome situations in their affairs. It is demanding yet hugely satisfying work, not without its challenges. The solutions I would help create were in the main incredibly simple. So simple in fact that one might wonder why highly talented people, better versed than I in their own industry or profession were unable to arrive at similar conclusions.

The answer to that is three-fold :

(a) It requires a detached perspective and a peculiarly imaginative mind-set to dream up sometimes unlikely remedies – there's few of us about!

(b) Practitioners in a particular business are often too close to situations to see the obvious

and

(c) Those brought up in a particular industry are so well groomed to following specific practices that the idea of working out-with them is regarded as impossible.

In both latter instances the core obstacle is that the

participants cannot or will not see and think 'outside the box'.

POWER POINT - *"The greatest obstacle to change in life or business is an inability or an unwillingness to 'think outside the box'."*

Add to that the fact that, because of the very reasons noted, many within businesses (and even those who hire you) can be hostile to what they see as unwarranted, uninformed, outside interference, then you start to realise that the work of a Creative Solutions Specialist is not nearly straightforward.

The key to overcoming such resistance is to involve obstructive individuals in the process of analysing situations and devising solutions so that they themselves become the change managers. Done well this often results in scenarios where former adversaries of your involvement not only embrace the change you've brought about but ultimately claim the credit for the finished work! If so ... fine. It is still job done!

Small Businesses and the Self-Employed

With successful small businesses and the self-employed there are two main circumstances which regularly occur and prompt proprietors to seek outside assistance. These are :

(a) Financial problems, most commonly caused by

• Insufficient earnings i.e. low sales

• Poor money management including lack of budgeting, reckless spending, excessive debt

- a variety of measures may be employed to counter these failings

and

(b) Quality of life issues. These mostly revolve around achieving (or not achieving as the case may be) a balance between working hard and earning profit and having the time to enjoy it.

As a classic case of 'quality of life issues' let's take as an example the highly successful family haulage business of 'Mick and Mary'. They have laboured hard and long years to grow their enterprise but now find that they have little or no family life, scant leisure time and, although financially well off, cannot see what benefit they derive from it. Less wealthy friends enjoy regular holidays and good times. Mick and Mary just go to work. They are tired.

After receiving their call I arranged a one hour introductory meeting with them. On the appointed day they arrived late, forty-five minutes into their allotted time. Animated and profuse, they gushed out a stream of business-related 'enforced justifications' (excuses) for their extreme tardiness. No apology – after all their business 'was more important'. After hearing them out I said the following :

"Mick and Mary you asked me here today because you are concerned with the intolerable pressure which your successful business is placing you under and you want to explore with me ways to reduce this stress and to improve your quality of life. So today, now, I am going to ask you one, just one question and then I am going to leave. After I have gone I want you to give serious thought to my question and see if you can come up with a truly meaningful answer. Please be totally honest with yourselves in doing so. Then, if as a result of your deliberation, you wish to arrange a further meeting with me, first pay my fee into this bank account *(I handed them the details)* and then call my assistant. Here is my question –

If you lack the organisation or discipline or determination to be present at the start point of your new road to happiness and freedom, if you are unable to put aside for just one hour the very work which is the root cause of your dissatisfaction, then do you honestly believe that you possess the commitment needed to drastically change your ways so as to improve your quality of life every day for the rest of your lives?"

- then I left.

Mick and Mary you see, successful as they were, had for years been putting the cart firmly before the horse, the well-being of their business ahead of their personal happiness.

Their behaviour regarding their meeting with me absolutely personified their great failing – that of *an inability to plan their business around their life;* instead randomly hoping that their life might just happen to fall into place around their business! Yes a business can create income and the profit from it can pay for life style ... but ... the business must be designed around the required life style, it must not exist at the expense of a quality life style.

POWER POINT - *"First determine your required life style and then design around it the business which will support it."*

Mick and Mary had also shown a lack of respect toward me. I had quickly comprehended that this emanated from their lack of respect for themselves and their own personal well-being.

Mick and Mary's answer to the question I posed them had to comprise first of an understanding that the cause of all their woes was their own negligence in duty of care to themselves. This personified by an inability to prioritise properly, time manage and plan ahead from the perspective of putting their own quality of life ahead of all else.

They had to accept that they were too close to their own situation to be able to understand how this objective might be achievable. They had to put their trust in me to devise and implement changes to their working practices which their industry knowledge would cause them to believe were not possible.

Many prospective clients of Creative Solutions Specialists never achieve this level of understanding. They do not find it possible to overcome their own resistance to what they perceive will be impossible change. Thus by default they remain chained to their treadmill of endless work.

Mick and Mary? They were among the successes. They did come up with the right answer to my question and they did arrange to see me again – arriving promptly too! Thereby overcoming their first hurdle. Together we did arrive at a happy and agreeable Creative Solution to their situation.

~

Most businesses, large and small, employ assets of different kinds within the enterprise. Two types of business asset are :

- *Fixed assets – property, machinery, vehicles, equipment*
- *Human assets – employees*

The purpose of employing assets such as these is to

increase the earning capability of the business and from that, hopefully, the profitability.

In fact for many businesses the assets are fundamental to the existence of the enterprise. A haulage contractor for example is a business wholly dependent on having trucks and drivers; a manufacturer needs premises, plant and most likely a work force.

Fixed Assets

In a perfect world the assets of a business would be fully paid for in cash at the outset. Unfortunately, in the vast majority of cases this is not so. Buildings will most often have a mortgage loan against them or be leased. Vehicles, plant and other equipment is more often than not on lease purchase, hired or party to some other credit arrangement.

This means that the earnings which the assets themselves help to create have to be substantial enough to cover the cost of the interest and credit repayments as well as meeting the other ongoing costs within the business.

As most machinery and vehicles are depreciating in value, with time there arises an increasing differential between the value of the assets and the servicing payments attached to them. (This may not always be the case with property which can experience increase in value long term).

It's a simple truth that a business without credit of any kind will always be better placed to be more competitive and more profitable than one with credit and, in bad times, much more able to 'weather the storm'. Businesses with credit on the other hand (the majority), tend to struggle more and are often the first to 'go under' when things get tough.

Human Assets

The same equation as referred to above generally applies to employees. While the cost of employees remains less than the earnings they create for the business then all is well but, when the amount that they earn for the business drops below the cost of their employment then that is when drastic steps such as making workers redundant have to be taken ... not good.

The Solution to the Cost of Assets

For the small business an ideal situation therefore would be to be able to enjoy all of the benefits of necessary assets (fixed and human) but while incurring none of the liability. Idyllic as this proposition might appear it is actually achievable. All that is required is a change in the way that the business is perceived by its owners!

Let's take as an example the haulage business mentioned before. It is absolutely dependent on possessing trucks and having drivers to drive them – right? Wrong!

The owners of the business, let's call them Mick and Mary, have slaved hard and long to establish their enterprise. They now have a fleet of trucks (all on credit), premises (on a mortgage) and drivers (all on wages). They are successful but long for a more relaxed life style free from the constant demands of debt and of the 'monster' they've created. How can they be set loose from the grip of their own business?

The answer lies within their own success! If they have grown the business as they have then they must have acquired the skill to find and to keep clients. It's a universal law. Regardless of how good your product or service in business may be, if you have no-one to supply it to then it is worthless.

POWER POINT - *"A business, even one with superb goods or service, is only as good as its ability to find clients."*

Therefore all businesses which prosper must by definition have become adept at sourcing clients (by whatever means) and keeping them. This skill is the key to Mick and Mary's hassle-free but profitable future.

Here's what they do :

- *They sell or lease out the business*
- *They retain the marketing rights and the branding (their trading name)*

Put another way, they dispose of all operational responsibility for the trucking business but they keep control of the marketing and of the client 'book'. They contract to be the sole and exclusive providers of marketing services in perpetuity to the new proprietors and to supply them with clients derived from their client base and their accumulated experience of finding business. They can offer the service to other haulage firms too. Mick and Mary have become *marketing consultants!*

So for Mick and Mary :

- *No trucks*
- *No premises*
- *No employees*
- *No debt*
- *Guaranteed income*
- *A life style free of all the operational hassle*

This model is applicable to any business in which the proprietors have mastered the art of client creation - *often referred to as* **sales and marketing!**

That is how to prosper in a business without the burden of the cost and hassle of the essential business assets!

Joseph T.Riach

Chapter 19

THE WOLF ON TRUTH STREET

I was drinking coffee with my friend Cavaco at his O Lobo café on Rua da Verdade (the Wolf on Truth Street)! It being both my duty and pleasure to support local business. This rather than visit a shopping mall or big brand franchise of those huge corporations which dominate both physical and online space. They getting ever richer while small traders and entrepreneurs are squeezed out of business. Besides, my neighbourhood café experience is friendly and fun. No amount of mega company ballyhoo can match the real flavours, value, camaraderie and social interaction of my 'local'. It's no contest.

That's why, as I looked down the largely deserted street from where we sat, I decided to buy the closed up flower shop next door. If I could add colour to the small corner of bustle which was the café then perhaps I could start to reverse the neglect of the community reflected in other empty shops and boarded up windows.

I recruited Lulu, 'the flower girl', to run things. She knew her stuff, so word of the flower shop soon got around. People started making detours from the larger centres. They told their friends, who told their friends and, before I knew it, a travel agent visiting from Lisbon spotted the derelict building next door and bought the lease. The premise was larger than he needed but, no problem. He opened a newsagent and tabacaria in the spare unit. Next to arrive was a grocer, then a hardware store, a hairdresser and a bakery. The town came alive! All done with personal initiative, industry and enterprise. And not a squeak from officialdom ... until ...

Word of the regeneration of the area reached the local council. A valuation surveyor was dispatched to re-evaluate the properties and businesses. An environmental impact study was ordered. Soon the businesses were flooded with inspectors, pointless regulations, meaningless paperwork, compliance notices and ... demands for duties and payments. Threats of legal action in the event of non-payment were attached.

Then national government weighed in demanding their slice of the action. This came by way of even more stringent regulations, licensing requirements and taxation – lots of it. All delivered in the name of working in the best interests of a community which, delighted with the thriving hubbub returned to their town, neither sought nor desired their interference.

Meanwhile, both local and central government, wheeled and dealed with the mega corporations, offering ludicrous incentives to devour green space and build ever more shopping centres. Their officials appearing to live in houses, drive cars and enjoy foreign travel far in excess of what even their self-awarded excessive salaries could possibly afford. The beleaguered small business owners financing these lifestyles inevitably concluded that the battle with the twin evils of bureaucracy and corruption was a losing one.

Lulu, the 'flower girl', was the first to quit. The travel agent and tobacconist soon followed suit. The grocer, hairdresser and bakery were next to go. The hardware store hung on for several months but the profit on a bag of screws or the occasional sale of a spirit level, eventually levelled the spirit of the proprietor and he too said 'screw this'. Only O Lobo survived.

Once again Cavaco and I thoughtfully regarded the deserted street from the viewpoint of his café terrace. That's when we decided to buy all the derelict properties. We drew up and submitted plans for a covered shopping precinct which retained all the original buildings and character. It consisted of a huge transparent dome over the entire street. Suddenly we were receiving ludicrous incentives, grants and public money to fund the venture.

We called our new arcade 'The Wolf on Truth Street Centre'. All the former traders returned plus a throng of local and other 'private enterprise only' businesses. The explosion of colour which greeted visitors on arrival was once more a prominent feature of the street. Yes, Lulu 'the flower girl' was back!

~

The Pakistani name Sikandar means 'A great king'. It derives from the Greek and is a reference to Alexander the Great of historical fame. For some time the name appeared distinctly inappropriate for .....

Sikandar was the oldest trainee at the accountancy college where his Pakistani family insisted that he study. He had little enthusiasm for the profession chosen for him. He studied little and became less a budding number cruncher and more a serial failure. While generations of bright, young students came, crammed, sat their exams, qualified and moved on to professional employment, Sikandar lazed disinterestedly on, failed his resits again and languished at college for yet another year. So long had he been repeating his seemingly endless cycle of failure that he earned the nickname of Pakitin as in, "Why don't you just pack it in?"

Had he done so, then the college would have lost not only the weary, weed-puffer, lolling half-asleep in class by day but also … the guy who threw the hottest weekend parties on campus! For what Sikandar lacked in enthusiasm for his purported profession he more than made up for in his passion for riotous living and cooking the meanest curries in town!

Each weekend his tiny, city centre apartment became home to his legendary beer 'n curry fests. What seemed like the town's entire student population cavorted there to an endless flow of iced beer and heaped bowls of steaming vindaloo. The throng spilled out on to the landing, the stairs and every apartment in the building. In any other block the neighbours would have raised hell at the blaring sitar and the heavy stench of curry, cannabis and joss sticks. But all the neighbours were at Sikandar's party too! On Saturday nights no-one suggested he should 'pack it in'. He became instead Pakemin! - as in 'pack them in'!

Sikandar never did pass his accountancy finals. The college authorities eventually resolved that a mid-aged, bohemian in their midst was not conducive to the general repute of the college. They 'let him go' – or packed him in, as he joked with friends.

He did find work as a 'junior' assistant in an uptown accountancy practice but was never entrusted with any meaningful responsibility. He spent his days exiled in a basement dungeon sifting through clients' cash receipts. When the firm's partners decided to sell off the basement, they were surprised when Sikander bought it. In true Pakistani tradition his family lent him the money. The accountants were even more surprised when he applied for, and despite their objections, was awarded a restaurant licence!

Sikandar wasted no time in setting up his eatery and recreating the ambiance of his student-days Saturday night curry fests. Diners loved it. Soon his restaurant was known as the 'hottest' spot in town. His personal place of joy and fulfillment was the kitchen. He cooked his heart out and once again served the meanest curry in town. Customers came from near and far to revel in the heady party atmosphere of his curry and beer extravaganzas; all consumed to the hypnotic and very loud beat of the sitar.

The accountants above, driven to distraction by the din when working nights and assailed by the rich curry aromas all day, eventually moved out. Sikandar purchased those floors of the building and converted them to restaurant too. When the renovations completed, he reopened as "Pakitin's Pak 'Em In Pakistani Joint"! The name created much hilarity when its origins were explained.

When diners congratulated him on the food, the vibrancy of his restaurant and inquired as to his inspiration, he would often reply,

"Did you permit someone other than yourself to choose food which you don't care for as your meal tonight or did you yourself select a dish which you really like?"

Then continued,

"So be it in life. Don't do as others insist, follow your passion and do what you love."

Then he would add with a sly grin,

"When you do that I can absolutely assure you that no-one, but no-one, will ever tell you to pack it in!"

~

Iain was anything but your normal city solicitor. Not only because of his fisher-folk family origins and traditions with accompanying dialect, both of which he steadfastly adhered to, but even more so because he maintained that his professional role was to help people rather than take advantage of them. To that end he would put the interests of his clients first and in his characteristically homely manner advise them in 'their language' as to their best, and least costly, courses of action; often divulging to them in the process what he saw as the less than proper practices of his colleagues which they should watch out for and avoid.

Not unexpectedly these factors put him at odds with the majority of his profession who saw him as a loose cannon and a threat to their established and lucrative practices.

But Iain was popular with the community at large, well respected for his practical and ethical approach and brought in a lot of business to the firm as a result. So the powers that be could not fire him, choosing instead to keep him 'on a leash', confined to a back office and without prospect of promotion.

None of this concerned Iain, for him it was a case of work as normal. Increasingly though he grew to loathe his profession and those immoral practitioners in it. He turned more and more to his past-time of practicing homeopathy. This work had always fascinated him and he derived great pleasure from it. He could see close up the benefits his homeopathy brought to his patients. He studied for his doctorate in the subject and in due course was able to abandon his legal career and indulge his true passion.

He bought an old country cottage in a rural village not far from the fishing town of his birth, close to his family and friends and the kinship of the local people. There Iain set up his homeopathy practice, discarded his striped suit and settled for a life of service to his community. Not a hugely profitable concern but a thoroughly satisfying one. One where he could truly help people rather than take advantage of them!

~

Margaret was the senior Middle-East correspondent for one of America's leading quality newspapers. A highly intelligent yet quietly spoken New Yorker, she became self-employed by necessity after being hounded from her employment during the McCarthy era. That time when accusations of communist subversion in high places was rife. Not that she was a communist nor a sympathiser. She simply refused to denounce colleagues as being so.

Angry and disillusioned, she relocated to London. There she set up on her own and continued her career as a freelance journalist; her knowledge and international reputation ensuring her of regular commissions from journals worldwide. In London she met Beryl who would become her companion and soulmate. Together they moved to south-west France. It was there that I met them.

In comparison to Margaret, Beryl was an unsophisticated character, a rough diamond with an abrasive edge. She called a spade a spade and had little time for social finery. After-dinner pleasantries were not for Beryl. It was with Margaret that I shared fascinating chat – not to mention quite a few bottles of good Bordeaux! - into the wee hours on many happy occasions. Time spent with Beryl was more likely to be when repairing machinery or renovating old properties, anything that involved dirty hands and vulgar language!

Yet, in spite of the huge difference in their personalities, their intellect and their likes and dislikes in life, Margaret and Beryl formed a perfect partnership. They were totally devoted to each other. Theirs was an unlikely alliance – but it worked!

This is the key point to note. It is neither necessary nor desirable to seek out relationships in life or business only with 'perfect' partners. A route to 'success' equally likely to produce positive results is to work with people of various backgrounds, skills, attitudes and ideas. Such arrangements bring more to the collective table.

I developed a lot of business this way. In early instances often unintentionally. But once I found myself working with, and benefiting from, people and situations of improbable diversity, I realised the advantages of such setups. I came to see that an unlikely alliance is frequently the most profitable. They are also most fun. So I actively sought out the rare and exotic, the eccentric and quirky to work with. So too should you. You'll be the more entertained, the more relaxed and the more richly rewarded through it.

Margaret's former employer degenerated over time into a partisan rag of third rate journalism. An environment with no place for journalistic integrity such as Margaret's. Their loss though was Margaret's, and the wider world's, gain. As a self-employed freelancer she enjoyed editorial independence and her career flourished. She found the love of her life and 'lived happily ever after' in the idyllic beauty of south-west France.

By becoming self-employed, forming an unlikely alliance and welcoming into her life the contrary, diverse, unusual and outrageous, Margaret turned misfortune into a golden opportunity. She dared to be different.

~

Work in my investment business was slow. With little to do, I left my office and drove downtown. The hand-painted "Noah's Ark Investments" sign outside a slightly shabby shop front caught my eye. Intrigued, I parked up and went inside.

"How can I help you young fella?" came the hearty greeting from a ruddy-faced gent lolling in an old rocker. I kind of liked the 'young fella' line so immediately felt at home.

"What's with the Noah's Ark Investments?" I queried, "This is an investment business, right ... ?" - my face screwed up in puzzled mode.

"Oh it's an investment business alright my friend," came the assertive reply, "But not just any investment business. It is *the* investment business, the genuine article, the real McCoy. You see, what I do here came around long before you or any slick greenhorns saw the light of day and it'll be here long after you're pushin' up daisies!"

"So what do you do?" I asked feeling well scolded, "And how come the odd name?"

"Nothin' odd about the name," he snapped back, "It says what it is. Clear and simple."

Then, leaning forward he indicated that I sit on the threadbare recliner at his side and added,

"Listen in an' you might learn something.

Old Noah of biblical legend was no fool," he started, "When he filled up that boat of his with two of every animal, he knew just what he was doing. He was investing in his future. Think about it lad."

Now I was a lad, even better! I eagerly leaned in to grasp the wisdom in prospect. It wasn't long in coming.

"In due course, each pair of animals reproduced. Then the offspring in turn did likewise. Soon he had herds of cattle and flocks of sheep. That was his capital growth."

He paused to let the significance of that revelation sink in. Then he continued,

"Some calves, lambs, chickens etc. he slaughtered. These gave him food, clothes and shelter. That was his income. Those he didn't kill grew into the herd or flock. That was his reinvesting his profit, his futures market if you like. And so the cycle continued. When he required something outwith of his own production capability, he bought and payed for it with a lamb, calf or chicken. That was his spending money."

So you see son," (wow, now I was his son, how could I not like this guy)!, "Noah was the original investor. His methods are tried and tested. There is nothing new to learn about investing. All you need do is follow his example. Think about it. Noah neither attended Harvard nor wolfed on Wall Street, he was much smarter than any of that."

Now my new friend beckoned to me and, with a conspiratorial wink, invited me to follow him. He led me to the back door and, throwing it open, revealed a back yard where gamboled several lambs, ducks and chickens.

"These are but a few, my full 'investment portfolio' is on the farm out of town," he laughed, "But I assure you young fella, good times and bad, they provide for my every need. More than that, what I do gives me, my family, my friends and my clients the greatest pleasure imaginable. Yes son, what I do is fun!"

"You recommend these 'investments' to clients?" I asked somewhat bemused.

"I surely do," he responded, "I recommend them, supply them and provide ongoing management advice. It's a full proactive portfolio management service. Yup," he slapped his thigh, "That's what I do," and let out a hearty laugh. I was deep in thought.

When I got back to my office some hours later, my PA was curious as to the cardboard cartons stacked in the back of my car. She was the more so incredulous when I explained it was my new investment portfolio and astounded when I showed her the rooster and six hens I had acquired.

Back home I built a wooden henhouse in the yard. Every day I collect the eggs, sometimes I roast a chicken. The flock grows with each hatch of chicklets. I sell some to fund my next investment - a piglet.

The "Noah's Ark Investments" sign I nailed above the henhouse door attracts a steady stream of inquirers. They in turn became my friends and promoters.

~

As late September's cooler breeze arrived, the tourists departed. I holdalled my flimsy summer wear and made to follow them. I lingered for a final beer at the tin shack beach bar which I had adopted as my author's study for several carefree weeks. It had proved ideal for my purpose. Young bartender Rui had kept me regularly refreshed as I scribbled in my 'private corner'.

A budding artist, Rui had painted one wall of the howff with cartoons of the bar and of all the other 'watering holes' on the waterfront too. The work was that of impassioned youth, painted with the loving attention to detail of one who had clearly enjoyed the hospitality of every one of the bars featured!

I could tell, as I had shared a similar love affair with drinking establishments during my formative years. Rui was eager to compare my story of misspent youth with his and to know how I found success. So I told him ...

"When Haggis, one of 'my gang' of friends left school, he went to work with the city council in the department which held the records of each and every business and residential property in the city and surrounds - and details of who occupied them. Haggis soon realised he had access to a list of every single pub, hostelry and drinking establishment in the region. Armed with this knowledge, 'our gang' set about the task of acquainting ourselves with, and downing ale, in every one of them. I'm ashamed to report that we succeeded rather admirably!

I did not become so pickled in the process however as not to learn several valuable lessons from my youthful excesses.

The first of these was to not spend all my money in pubs. The second was how to make money from the time I did spend in pubs! Yes, I turned my teenage tomfoolery into meaningful business. How did this come about? - simple.

When I got to setting up my own business, I used Haggis's register of pubs and the names of their owners and landlords as a ready made target niche of potential customers. I surveyed them to find which goods and/or services best appealed to them, then supplied just that.

I also recruited several of the bar owners as my agents. They promoted my services in their premises and to their customers, and they referred me to their clients. It was a perfect set up.

So perfect in fact that I hired an assistant to research more of the public records pertaining to property in the town. Soon, I could identify the owners and/or tenants and occupiers of almost every city property. I subdivided these into niches according to area, type of property (business or residential), business practiced or trade/profession and circumstances of occupier etc. and then researched and defined which goods and services were most appropriate to which niche. Then, and only then, did I create an enterprise appropriate to the particular niches.

By repeating this formula I created over time many successful businesses. So the lesson for you Rui is to do likewise. Turn your delinquent days passion - the beach, the bars, your art - into your adult years income. That way you will have fun and always make money too. I'll write down my formula for you just in case you forget!"

I grabbed a paper napkin and scribbled the following :

1. Have fun.

2. Turn your fun into income.

3. Use your local knowledge and public records to research your market – do your homework!

4. Tailor your offering to suit the potential buyers you have identified – not the other way around.

5. Involve your clients as partners too.

I handed Rui the slip, downed my beer and we hugged the hug of a happy summer shared. Then I headed for home.

It may have been the end of summer but the day marked the start of Rui's successful beach bar and art gallery chain of eateries. It also marked the completion of my first best-selling book. A plaque at 'my' table in what is today Rui's Bar reads -

"This is where Joseph Tom Riach wrote 'Mastering The Art Of Making Money'. Read it and prosper. I did! - Rui."

A nearby stand displays all my books for sale. Rui and I are each in our own way practicing exactly what I preached!

From our respective entrepreneurial positions we firmly agree that every day is opportunity, every day a new beginning. From that perspective, every day is sunny and fun-filled. The end of summer? ... there's no such thing!

~

You can take Cavaco's, Sikandar's, Iain's, Margaret's, Noah's and Rui's stories literally (all are fact based) or allegorically. It doesn't matter. The approach is the same. Identify the opportunity, follow your passion, think and act with clarity. Avoid the complex. The obvious is most often staring you in the face.

For example - As an investment consultant I worked out the Noah strategy for myself. I abandoned the bamboozle-you schemes my host investment companies wanted me to promote and made myself rather unpopular with them by simply recommending 'Noah'.

As unpopular as I became with the companies, I became hugely popular with clients. I 'sold' to every single prospect who approached me and earned massively in the process.

It's a story I relate to all my visitors and anyone else who wants to know. Those who don't want to know, are the poorer for it. It's why I derive great amusement from the plethora of 'make a fortune' schemes I see touted around. You don't need to be a genius to see through them.

In life you need only be a Harry Barclay, a Cavaco, a Sikandar, an Iain, a Margaret, a Noah, a Rui – or me - simple!

Joseph T.Riach

Chapter 20

THE ART OF SMART

Y ou should know by now that success in life or business is just not possible without the application of single minded determination and simple hard work. The two are essential to any meaningful degree of achievement. Yet, there is another trait which, when added to the mix, raises you to a different level altogether, makes you unbeatable. To truly succeed at the very highest level, you must - master the art of working smart!

POWER POINT - *"Work hard at working smart!"*

What is working smart? What does it mean? Well, in my book there are three categories of work -

* Hard Work – Typically dealing with crises, pressing issues, deadlines, meetings and interruptions. Rushing around a lot and being very important.

* No Work – Attending to some mail, phone calls, popular activities, trivia, games and time wasters. Procrastinating.

and

* Smart Work - Smart workers spend time on Preparation, Planning, Prevention, Relationship Building, Personal Development, Enjoying Life – AND - they employ their Native Wit!

There are in fact two distinct aspects to *working smart :*

Native Wit and ***Work Practices***

Of the two, native wit is natural and devastatingly effective. Most people who are employing it didn't learn it. They do it intuitively, it's part of their character, of who they are and how they were raised. Within this book, Harry Barclay is the perfect example. But you can aspire to be like Harry and those others endowed with native wit by -

* Altering the way you think, your attitudes

and

* Consciously applying appropriate life and work practices

To do so you'll need to give consideration to the following. No smart worker has all of them, but the more elements you manage to include into your working strategy and style, the smarter the worker you will become :

Put yourself first

Think before you act

Know what you want

Ask for what you want

Control your emotions

Be innovative and bold

Be in the right businesses

Look on the bright side of life

Know and play to your strengths

Employ good life management skills

Employ good time management skills

Identify and act on the right opportunities

Create intellectual products and/or services

Provide a scarce resource into a high demand market

Additionally you should –

Leverage other people's time and money

Hang out with only the best people

Know when to cut your losses

Keep things in perspective

Network and ask for help

Create and deliver value

Be nimble minded

Be Flexible

and

Be generous, compassionate and kind!

Working smart means finding your strengths and knowing your weaknesses as opposed to the *'doing it all yourself and burn out'* of working hard.

It also means maintaining your personal integrity and never involving yourself in anything which diminishes you or goes against your personal values.

Above all else, working smart means knowing your self worth and never under selling yourself intellectually or financially.

POWER POINT - *"Value yourself highly, intellectually and financially."*

The idea of working smarter rather than working harder is not, of course, new. While it's easy to explain what working harder is – starting early, longer hours, staying late – it's far more difficult to define working smart.

In the case of the Harry Barclays of the world it is almost indefinable. It's an intangible entity, a state of mind, a way of thinking, a god given gift. However, one thing is certain. He and the others like him have an incredibly simple and intuitive way of seeing things. To put it the other way around, they do not see or recognise complexity in anything. They blank out complexity and are the smarter for it. *They are astoundingly quick at seeing the obvious.*

POWER POINT - *"Keep everything simple. Blank out complexities. See what is in front of your eyes."*

While working hard entails much work, it is work which is not necessarily going to make a lot of difference. Smart work on the other hand makes a substantially bigger, and usually far speedier, impact.

To work smart :

* Focus on only those things which actually move you forward in life.

* Separate out mundane tasks and delegate them to others.

* Create disciplined but fun schedules with regular breaks.

* Do the hardest things first and early in the morning while your brain is fresh and alert.

* Don't procrastinate or do tasks only partially. Start them *now* and see them through to completion.

* Be selective about doing only genuinely high pay off activities.

* Plan your activities ahead, rehearse as necessary.

* Remember too that enthusiasm should be tempered with wisdom. Consider beforehand, and at your leisure, all the details of whatever it is that you are contemplating so you can be sure that everything will be accomplished without fuss, on time and accurately.

* At the point of involvement, focus on fun elements and enjoying what you are doing.

* Avoid complex situations and people. Sticking to simple works.

* Work out ways to make tasks easier or delegate them to others.

* *The importance of 'No'.* There is no single ability which constitutes working smart than saying *"No"* when you need to.

Whether in personal life or in business, there is no benefit in taking on un-necessary work, allowing others to be unrealistic in their expectations of you or simply having people take advantage of your good nature. In order to dedicate yourself to the important aspects of your life and business you must know when to say, and be confident in saying, "No" to things which contribute nothing to your well-being or to the achievement of your objectives.

Practice by saying "No" to as many people as possible, as often as possible. Do it just for the hell of it! You'll feel great. Saying 'no' is saying 'yes' to owning your own future.

POWER POINT - *"Saying 'no' is saying 'yes' to owning your own future."*

In reality, not just this chapter, but the entire content of this book is about working smart. All of the guidance, suggestions and examples are about urging you to do just that; to dare to be different, to own your own future, to think and work smart.

The alternative is not appealing. It is to stay bogged down in the same rut as everyone else, as all those who are not daring to be different and are not determined to own their own futures. Where's the point or the excitement in that?

The main barrier to progressing as individuals and taking control of their lives which so many face is in their mindset, their attitude. When they encounter someone different to themselves, someone self-confident and in control, they become confused. They think that the difference is due to a freak of birth or some other cruel trick of nature to which they have been subjected. Therefore they look for the 'secrets' of the smart thinkers in ever more complex areas. Yet the very opposite is the truth.

Those who work smart generally follow very simple life and business practices. So simple in fact that the majority of people cannot see or will not believe that these practices are at the very heart of the smart thinkers' success. Did you, for example, find anything complicated with the stories of Cavaco, Sikandar, Iain, Margaret, Noah or Rui? Does anything about Harry Barclay's approach confuse you?

It's somewhat like the clue to the murder sitting on the mantelpiece. No-one expects it to be there, so no-one finds it. They search every nook and cranny, upturn every stone. To no avail. Yet all the time the answer is right there before their eyes. So with the art of working smart. It is simple activities carried out repetitively and well which mount up to great achievements. This is the single most powerful 'secret' of the smart worker!

POWER POINT - *"Simple activities carried out repetitively and well are what mount up to great achievements."*

Yet this is what so many cannot or will not see. Before you can become a master the art of smart, it will be necessary for you to learn to think the way that smart thinkers do. This will usually involve a process of **uneducating** from your mind many well entrenched beliefs and practices.

POWER POINT - *"Learning to work smart will not be easy. Be prepared to uneducate yourself from thinking and working in complex ways."*

As very young children we mostly all display a high level of native wit. A range of natural thought processes and actions designed to allow us to live successfully in the wild. Modern society sanitises out much of this through our culture and education. By the time most people reach their twenties, they have totally capitulated to the expectations of society and to the peer pressure of the majority. They are thinking and acting just like the rest of the population who display, in all their thoughts and actions, a desperate desire to be equal in mediocrity. Don't let this be you!

Make it your aim to tap into the reservoir of native wit which still resides deep within you. Listen to your gut instinct. Work smart.

Joseph T.Riach

Chapter 21

THE MORE YOU HAVE FUN

The roar of the crackling log fire in the hearth of the country inn was matched only by the drinkers' hearty roars of laughter as they reacted to a local fisherman's colourfully embroidered yarn of 'the one that got away' - the size of the elusive salmon magically increasing with every telling. I swigged my pint and joined in the general revelry.

The fun story of a frustrating day of fruitless casting by the riverbank also caused me to reflect on my own experience of a quite different kind of fisherman's tale - the one that tells of extreme hardship and danger in the hostile environment of deep-sea trawling.

The hardy souls who inhabit that world have no need of bragging rights when recounting their high seas adventures. Every one of them knows that the real-life deprivation and risk of their occupation far surpasses any improbable yarn dreamt up in the cosy surroundings of a wayside tavern. Trawlermen's howffs are bawdy dockside bars where they drink to erase, not recall, their most awful memories and to dim the perilous prospects of their next voyage.

Those of the crews who do not shipwreck on booze when ashore tend to be introspective, they speak little of their life at sea. Many lead quiet lives and cherish their time at home with family. 'Skipper Jim' was one such softly spoken man. He lacked the rugged features and vulgar nature of many seamen but was no less hard as lobsters' claws through it.

Jim 'treated' me to my one and only experience of life as a deep-sea trawlerman. The two week winter voyage to the North Atlantic fishing grounds in search of cod, halibut, herring and haddock proved to be one of the most chastening experiences of my young life. At fifteen and fit, I considered myself to be as tough as they come. How wrong I was!

As the veritable 'boy among men' I was worked to the bone. After just two days my hands were chaffed red raw from hauling cables, cleaning nets, manhandling boxes, shoveling ice and gutting fish. I was given every toughest, filthiest and most dangerous job going.

This included a terrifying clamber to secure the radio antenna at the top of the mast in a fearsome gale, driving sleet and heaving seas. I rarely slept. Whenever I did steal a moment to rest my battered body in a cramped box bunk, I was inevitably immediately awoken with the cry that the nets were being cast again - a fresh shoal of fish had been detected on the sonar.

I was the constant butt of the crew's jokes. They nicknamed me 'Tom Thumb'. Not that I was small in stature but because I was short on experience, knowledge and, most of all, the stamina of body and spirit with which they, to a man, abounded. Some boasted impressive physiques but mostly they were wiry individuals, tough as the seamen's thigh-high boots they wore and impervious to anything that man or nature could throw at them. They laughed, joked and leg-pulled incessantly. Humour was the bedrock of their existence. I've never forgotten that.

Through the trawlermen I understand that there is no situation in which I might find myself in life which remotely compares to the discomfort and danger of their harsh life at sea. If they can laugh in the face of such daunting adversity, then I know that I can easily find fun in far less demanding circumstances. As an entrepreneur, business or self-employed person, you would be wise to do likewise.

~

I love a good laugh and taking your work seriously doesn't mean you can't have fun. You'll stay in better condition, physically and mentally, when you ensure that your business does not take you over and provoke stress. In fact, you'll find that life and everything in it goes that much better when you and those around you are all having a good time. I believe that the more you have fun, the more you'll get done.

There's pleasure to be got from overcoming difficulties, shifting the inevitable stumbling blocks you encounter in your life or enterprise and finding innovative way to circumvent them. I myself just feel so goddam privileged to be there in the ring and fighting that I don't have time to not enjoy myself. That's why you'll find me slaving away at my work (enjoying myself) long after everyone else has gone to the pub, gone home and gone to bed! I don't want to miss a second of the high spirits I experience in every waking moment.

I say 'experience', that's true, but I create the levity. It's not accidental. I provoke it at every turn. Those unfamiliar with me and seeing me at work often don't suspect that I am working at all! I can be perceived as a carefree nonchalant by the casual observer and certainly not as someone diligently engrossed in a demanding endeavour.

Yet, as with all of life, the harder you work at what you do, the more you practice and prepare then, when the time to 'perform' arrives all the hard graft has been done. You are free to express yourself with confidence, relaxed in the knowledge that the more you are enjoying yourself the more you are impressing your abilities on the people and situations around you.

Your behaviour may put you at odds with others in your trade or profession but that's of no consequence. What does matter is that you are content, those working with you are happy and productive and clients see in you a good-humoured professional who produces outstanding results. Everyone is happy.

Try it for yourself –

The more you have fun, the more you'll get done!

~

Here is a bit of fun to finish with – but it's serious too! I call it '*the trick to making money*'. This is what you must do :

Put one dollar under a hat. Tap the hat three times with your magic wand and say the magic words – "*I am wealthy*". Lift the hat and voila! ... you will find that there are now two dollars.

Leave one dollar under the hat and put the other under a second hat. Repeat the magic process with that hat – tap it three times with your magic wand and say the magic words, "*I am wealthy.*" Lift the hat and find that you now have two dollars there.

Leave one dollar under that hat and put the other dollar under a third hat. Repeat the process as before and then again and again until you have nine hats each with one dollar underneath them plus you have your original dollar to hand. You have now turned your one dollar into ten. Fantastic!

Now, split your nine dollars of gain into *three pools* of *three* dollars each.

* *Pool One* is **spending money** – enjoy your profit and live a little!

* *Pool Two* is to be **saved** - hold on to your new wealth. This is very important. The power of money lies in having it.

* *Pool Three* is to create **further growth** ... so .....

Place those three dollars under a hat. Tap the hat three times with your magic wand, say the magic words, "*I am wealthy,*" and voila! ... you will find that there are now six dollars under the hat!

Now continue the process as before, placing three dollars of gain under successive hats until you have nine hats each with three dollars under them. That's twenty-seven dollars of gain. Plus your starting three dollars. That's thirty dollars – plus the three dollars spend and three dollars saved from the first round and of course your original one dollar. You now have thirty-seven dollars in total.

Add nine of these dollars to each of your spend and save pools. Add the starting three dollars to your original one dollar to create -

* *Pool Four* – a fund for **helping out less fortunate folks.**

Next? You've guessed it – take the remaining nine dollars and repeat the nine hat sequence. With that sequence complete you'll have one hundred and twenty-eight dollars in total. Split it into the pools as before. Then keep on repeating the nine hat routine for as long as you feel inclined to or until you're sick of the sight of money (or hats) – whatever. This is the trick to making money.

Part of the 'magic' is that growth of the reinvested money accelerates exponentially through the power of compounding. But, before you can benefit from compounding, you must first have cash to compound. For most folks that money must first be earned. And to work profitably requires knowledge of your business, being excellent at what you do. That in turn takes learning, training and practice.

Therefore to perform the trick of making money, the sequence to follow is :

First : Gain the knowledge to succeed – that's your *magic hat*.

Second : Work with excellence on your endeavour – that is your *magic wand*.

Lastly : Repeat the *magic words*, "*I am wealthy.*" – that is programming your subconscious to make success inevitable.

All of which leaves just one question. How to make the original one dollar into two dollars? It can be done in many ways and surprisingly easily. Think about all that you have read in this book. Make a list of ways to double the dollar, then select your preferred strategy. Regardless of the method you choose, one thing is certain. You'll do it most easily when you are self-employed.

Being your own boss – that's the real trick to making money!

CONCLUSION

HANGING OUT IN HEAVEN
A Final Thought From The Author

Self-employment is, more than anything, an adventure! It's an adventure which can transport you to the heights of happiness. And it will – provided that you heed and practice the following guiding principles. They are not what you might expect :

* Your over-riding aim in your self-employment should be to achieve a state of tranquility and calm, an awareness of life's simple treasures and to feel constant gratitude for them

* To fully appreciate life in that way, you must make kindness to others your priority

* Through kindness and generosity to others, wealth in your commercial pursuits will find you

* It is necessary to experience financial wealth in order to properly appreciate that it does not constitute, nor can it buy you, happiness

* Once thus aware then you can put aside material ambition and achieve a state of tranquility and calm .... and so the circle completes.

This journey of life is one in which you will inevitably experience joy and disappointment, pain and pleasure, success and failure. That's how an adventure should be. Live the day and let the outcome take care of itself. You'll do just fine as long as your attitude remains positive, upbeat and optimistic in all circumstances. Attitude is everything!

When sometimes reflecting on the paths taken, and not taken, in my life, three thoughts occur to me.

The first is that, despite an extensive back catalogue of folly, willfulness and sheer stupidity, I harbour very few regrets.

The second is that, if I find myself at this stage of life's journey in a shady nook by a babbling brook rather than in a monster infested dark forest, then this cheerful state has little to do with foresight on my part but everything to do with mindset.

Alas, I could not see clearly the way ahead much of the time nor forecast outcomes. I could however choose to set my mind on a positive course. This commenced with the realisation that I was no genius. This admission of my own ignorance marked the beginning of my wisdom!

I saw in those who displayed the trait, that modesty is marvelous and a rare quality. As a result I determined to allow no controversy into my life nor permit others to engage me in theirs. Nor do I choose to forcefully express opinions. I feel that it matters not that others know of, or agree with, what I do or do not believe. It matters only that I honour my beliefs.

Which brings me to my third thought - that central to what does matter is having confidence in my own integrity; nurturing, protecting and projecting it. This entails listening to my inner spirit, thinking accordingly, saying what I think and doing what I say. It may seem like a tall order but exercising integrity in your life becomes easier the more that you do it. Eventually, behaving thus is second nature. It's also fun and feels good! It is this which has allowed me to live my dream of a perfect life. A life of hanging out in heaven .....

My friend Zé lazed back in his rickety wicker chair. He exhaled a perfect ring of blue smoke from his inhalation of aptly named Disque Bleu cigarette and replied,

"Hanging out in heaven of course."

Then he smiled contentedly and said nothing. He eyed me as the crazed foreigner which I so clearly was. He had a point. I had asked him 'What was he doing here?' ... then instantly regretted it. His response confirmed the inanity of my question.

Zé had been a cordon bleu trained chef, preparing quality cuisine for discerning diners in posh restaurants ... before giving it all up and becoming a beach bum. For the ten years preceding our conversation he had lived in a makeshift, tarpaulin and orange-box shack on a small island in the lagoon surrounding where we sat.

He lived off fresh fish caught on his 'doorstep', occasional 'donations' from tourists who he regaled with lurid tales of his 'life and adventures' living rough in southern Portugal and 'contributions' of wine, coffee and anything else from local acquaintances such as myself.

At that moment we were sipping a rather pleasant Borba I'd brought along to while away a couple of hours chatting in the early evening sunshine. Soon we were joined by Jarvis.

"I heard that," Jarvis volunteered as he appeared through the sand dunes, "It was a dumb question." I shrugged in agreement.

"What else are we doing, you, me, all three of us, if not hanging out in heaven?" he commented.

"Mind you," he added, as he plumped himself on the pile of driftwood which constituted Zé's 'guest' chair and turned his attention to his 'host',

"My idea of heaven is somewhat more refined than yours. How you can live in this midden … ," here he swept an outstretched arm around at the junk of Zé's existence, " … beats me. I like the natural life, sure I do, but I need my creature comforts too."

Jarvis did indeed like his creature comforts. Home to him was a spacious villa with extensive grounds in an affluent neighbourhood. It was lavishly furnished and boasted a sauna, large swimming pool and tennis court. He wore designer brand clothes, drove an expensive sports coupé and dined regularly in the same upmarket restaurants where Zé had formerly worked. The two had in fact met many years past while Jarvis was eating in a 'Zé restaurant'. They had remained friends since. I sat back and tuned in to their good-natured banter.

It occurred to me listening to them that both men were, most assuredly, 'hanging out in heaven'. For that matter, so was I. Yet our concepts of that heaven varied considerably. Yes, the physical world we shared was the same. We inhabited the same blissful, geographical location. But how we each chose to experience our existence there differed greatly.

Zé had experienced the 'high life', then gave it up in

favour of an ultra simple, non-materialistic world in which only the 'today' mattered.

Jarvis continued to pursue and enjoy all the trappings of affluence and the hectic social whirl surrounding it.

For me, the peace, tranquility and freedom of my 'heaven' reigned supreme.

As I drained my cracked clay mug of the last of my wine, I bade my farewells to my two friends, still cackling merrily by Zé's camp fire, and wandered home.

I reflected that 'hanging out in heaven' meant different things to different people. More so than anything, it is not so much governed by your physical presence or location. Rather, it is a choice you make, a choice which comes from and resides within you. In that respect anyone can be 'hanging out in heaven' anywhere, any time.

It's not a case of you hanging out in heaven. It's a case of choosing to have heaven hanging out in you!

~

Read all about Tom, his work and his latest publications at www.tomriach.com

Joseph T.Riach

POWER POINTS

Every chapter of this book is based on my own real life experiences and each one contains what I consider to be essential guidance as to how to most rewardingly conduct your life, business and self-employment. Points I consider to be of particular significance are highlighted as *Power Points*.

They are listed again here for your quick reference; plus I've thrown in a few other gems of wisdom from my other works. Read them, memorise them, employ them. They will serve you well.

The Secret World Of Self-Employment

"Are you doing what you love doing?"

"Doing what you love always benefits other people too."

"Create your business to meet your own needs first."

"Become the limited supply in a market in which there is huge demand."

"Aim to provide only best in class, well prepared goods or services."

"Ask for what you want. Ask for the business."

"To be master of your own destiny you must become your own boss."

"There is no single ability which constitutes working smart than saying, *"No"*

"The words Duty, Freedom, Honour, Hope, Justice, Mercy; sum up what it is to be human."

"Lead by example."

"Lots of money equals 'choice' and 'power'."

"Zero-risk in life is not an option!"

"Live the you that is your brand!"

"Always get paid ahead of doing the work."

"Working smart is critical to success."

"Let someone else take the risk."

"Let others take the heat … you take the profit!"

"Have a definitive long term goal – employ short term analytics and flexibility."

"You don't need a 'Klondike situation' in order to prosper as an entrepreneur!"

"Dare to be different. Being the same as others means at best being mediocre."

"Summon up the courage to defy convention and follow your own instincts and gut feelings."

"Generosity should flow from the heart and be enriching to both donor and recipient."

"Say what you feel and do what you say."

"Swallowing your pride and asking for help takes courage. Not asking shows a lack of humility."

"You never know 'til a dead horse kicks you."

"Never underestimate the wisdom and wit of the common man."

"Striving each day to be the best that you can be is the best that you can be!"

"Small changes bring huge rewards."

"Choose to pursue your dream and do the thing you most enjoy."

"Make every day your best day."

"Tell yourself every day – 'Today is the best day of my life' – then go about making it so."

"Make time for physical exercise to sharpen your body – and mind!"

"Live a relaxed life to produce higher quality results and more of them."

"Snickling all day makes for fun, rest and play!"

"Trust your gut feelings, they will serve you well."

"To fully experience life, push yourself to your limit - and then a bit more."

"Do not assume responsibility for the envy and greed of those too lazy to create their own wealth."

"The pessimist sees difficulty in every opportunity; the optimist sees the opportunity in every difficulty."

"Great achievers share the common personality traits of vision, determination and self-belief."

"You are the richest man on earth — you just have to be smart enough to know it."

"What is lovely to one person is lousy to another. Perception of beauty is related to personal circumstance."

"What you put into life is what you'll get out."

"Your thoughts of today build your life of tomorrow."

"Life is not about perfection, enjoy what you have for as long as you have it."

"Don't let what you can't have spoil your enjoyment of what you do have."

"Everything comes to he who waits."

"If in doubt defer."

"Act on impulse, follow your gut instinct and enjoy a life of excitement, spontaneity and fun."

"Only some of your efforts will lead to success but all those ideas you don't act on will certainly fail."

"Use your smartphone selectively and only for constructive and appropriate tasks."

"Live life in the present moment by being present in your real life with real people."

"The bulk of smartphone traffic is non-essential and access to it not an immediate requirement."

"Laughter starts at home – both physically within the family and personally within yourself."

"Laugh at yourself and grant others the right to laugh at and with you too."

"If I can laugh at you, you can laugh at me and we'll all laugh together!"

"Be exceptional, create only feel good days. Bad days are not acceptable."

"Kick the losers out of your life - and leave them out!"

"You already know within you what is right and what is wrong."

"Every day in every way I'm getting better and better!"

"The more I have fun, the more I get done!"

"I am kind and generous every day!"

"Today is my best day ever!"

"Always use upbeat, enthusiastic language. It's infectious. Everyone responds to it."

"Feed your integrity with positive thoughts and generous actions. Show your happiness to the world."

"Successful human beings accept sole responsibility for their own thoughts, actions and the consequences of them."

"Be true to yourself and earn the respect which your integrity merits."

"Only the present moment is real – relax and enjoy it."

"Implant positive beliefs in your inner psyche with repeated assertions of your strengths and achievements."

"Practice daily self critique and daily self love too. Be self aware."

"Have the courage to say what you think and show your true emotions."

"Create great relationships by recognising your own emotions and acknowledging other peoples'."

"When you shut down one emotion, you shut down them all."

"Struggling with and denying your emotions simply leads to more suffering."

"Ignoring or suppressing your emotions risks losing your identity and self-respect."

"Processing and experiencing your feelings is part of leading a full life."

"Why would you treat yourself with less care and affection than you would afford to a special friend or loved one?"

"Create situations so that you control the risk or eliminate it."

"Own your own future. Entrepreneurs beat the drum, they don't follow the band."

"Ignore others' worthless comments and go your own way."

"Never trust an 'expert'!"

"Only by being adventurous can you possibly gain."

"Entrepreneurs are leaders."

"Your passion and self-belief must be absolute in order to succeed in self-employment – or any area of life."

"Be a risk taker – and bold with it."

"Ask directly and spell out exactly what it is that you want from people and situations."

"Be focussed and unshakable in your pursuit of excellence but flexible and resilient too."

"Laugh at yourself. Take your work seriously but never yourself. People don't like self-importance."

"You might have the finest goods or service on offer but unless you can sell them then you'll go nowhere – fast!"

"Whatever other business disciplines you may excel in, you will only reach your full potential when you master selling."

"Be prepared to have informed conversations with customers while displaying your in-depth, specialist knowledge."

"Being your own boss and having the duty of instilling motivation and discipline on yourself is harder by far than managing other people. Fail on this and your business fails."

"Everyone loves laughter and everyone loves you when you create it."

"There is education in school and college and there is education on the street. Seek out and master them both."

"The hard work in life or business is in the preparation."

"Trust your gut instinct. It will serve you well."

"Successful achievers possess and exercise relentless self-discipline."

"In life and business keep all things simple, work determinedly and avoid un-necessary expense."

"The more you have fun, the more you'll get done!"

"Choose to do only work which you truly enjoy and which helps other people."

"Let your passion determine your niche and then both will define your success."

"Try this and that; find your passion; establish your niche."

"To be the best, work only with the best."

"Compete by not competing. Think outside the box. Find innovative ways to get to clients first. Make an exclusive offer."

"Would you rather do business with someone pushy who you don't know or with someone trustworthy who you do know?"

"If you want higher self-esteem then find ways to boost someone else's self esteem."

"If you want to raise your positive spirit then assist someone else to raise theirs."

"If you want more happiness in life the smartest way to get it is to help someone else achieve it."

"Stand out from the crowd."

"The assertive and persistent succeed in business, the weak-willed fail."

"Do not assume risk or liability on someone else's behalf."

"Seek situations where the risk is minimal and/or shared and personal gain is substantial."

"You are not in business to be popular. Success comes from being respected."

"Be determined to persevere!"

"Successful entrepreneurs 'get on their bike' and speak to prospects and clients face to face."

"Do your market research and target your promotional work to the niche where your buyers are."

"Never think that success comes work free. Waiting for success is a long wait."

"You can prosper as an entrepreneur in any environment anywhere."

"A bad attitude is like a flat tyre. You won't get anywhere until you change it."

"Opportunity is seeing a solution to a difficulty."

"Do your selling yourself. You're the best person for it."

"Never let anyone have access to your cash."

"Better to employ no-one at all rather than someone you don't trust."

"Stand out from the crowd."

"Turn difficult situations into winning ones."

"Impress people with the simple excellence of your work."

"Reverse psychology – do or be the opposite of what people expect."

"Do not judge a book by its cover."

"Neither look up to the rich nor down on the poor."

"Perform – but perform as a better version of yourself."

"Presentation is everything!"

"Entrepreneurs are inventive risk takers who look for new ways to do things."

"Use loss leaders and incentivise customers with novel offers."

"Know your niche and develop your brand to appeal to it."

"Inventive entrepreneurs create their own market trends."

"Know everything about your industry, the people in it and all that is going on."

"Successful entrepreneurs never buy then sell, they first sell and then buy!"

"Buy only at absolute rock bottom dollar."

"Be ruthless in business but generous in life."

"You are your own biggest enemy – aim to be the best in the business."

"Know inside out your market, your place in the market and your competitors."

"Look within, look outwith, act on what you see."

"Don't trash the competition. Focus on, and speak about, what you do well."

"Act decisively to replace staff, clients and contracts when they become no longer useful, productive or profitable."

"Concentrate your efforts on sales and money management. Negligence of these are the biggest killers to businesses."

"Always work to a properly assessed business plan with ongoing oversight and management."

"Go big on market research, it's money well spent."

"Innovators and contrarians create change and shape destiny."

"Those who are offended by your humour don't matter and those who matter in your life won't be offended."

"With responsibility comes rights and vice versa. You cannot have one without the other."

"Your integrity is your most valued possession. Guard it well."

"Keep personal and sole control of the keys of your business – always."

"Grab opportunities. Acting impulsively on gut feeling can often pay off handsomely."

"Good fortune can embrace an unplanned project."

"Strive to create the most from the least."

"Work only with people who accept payment as you do, on a performance only basis."

"Don't pass up on opportunities. Just say 'Yes'!"

"Sell! The finest product or service is useless unless you can sell it."

"Work to be the best sales person ever. It will pay you handsomely."

"Make your business a pay up front one – or get into a business which is. No exceptions."

"Grab zero outlay opportunities and make them pay big time."

"Always ask for what you want and always deliver on what you promise."

"Complication is often a form of deception. A dustbin lid is a dustbin lid regardless of what you call it."

"Be true to yourself - live life, laugh and love."

"Work hard at working smart!"

"Value yourself highly, intellectually and financially."

"Keep life simple. Blank out complexities. Trust what you see."

"Saying 'no' is saying 'yes' to owning your own future."

"Working smart can produce absolutely free, everything for nothing, zero cost business projects."

"Simple activities carried out repetitively and well are what mount up to great achievements."

"Learning to work smart will not be easy. Be prepared to uneducate yourself from thinking and working in complex ways."

"Live to be different and to make a difference."

"Master the art of working smart."

"Own your own future. Be self-employed!"

Joseph T.Riach

RESOURCES

My thanks go to all the valuable sources of information, inspiration, motivation - and trivia too – referred to in these pages. All have been of real value, not just to me in writing this book, but also to all those who work with me. Readers of all my books and guests on my life and business coaching courses also benefit hugely from the various material. I am confident that you will also.

Literature

Homecoming – *John Bradshaw*

Mastering the Art of Making Money – *Joseph T.Riach*

Schindler's Ark – *Thomas Keneally*

Self Improvement Should Be Fun! – *Joseph T.Riach*

The Bible - *Various*

The Collected Works of Carl Jung – *Carl Jung*

The Simplest Sales Strategy – *Joseph T.Riach*

The Works of Lord Byron – *George Gordon Byron*

The Works of Mark Twain - *Mark Twain*

Tom Thumb – *Anon, origin 16th century English folklore*

Too Early For A Glass Of Wine? - *Joseph T.Riach*

Winning Big In Life And Business – *Joseph T.Riach*

Online

Author's Press Releases – *ibosocial.com/wakeup2wealth*

Author's Web Site – *www.tomriach.com*

Films

Schindler's List - *Co-producer and director Steven Spielberg, writer Steven Zaillan based on the novel by Thomas Keneally. Academy Award Best Film 1994*

Quotes

"A man who acquires the ability ….. " - *Andrew Carnegie*

"A song, a dance and a silly walk" - *Max Wall*

"Look after yourself ….. " - *my Mum*

"My word is my bond" - Anon

"Presentation!" - *Oskar Schindler*

"Take your work seriously but never yourself" - *Anon*

"Taken with a pinch of salt" - *Anon, from Roman times*

"Too good a chance to miss" - *Chic Murray*

Sources of Inspiration

Alexander the Great – Alexander III of Macedonia, 356 to 323 BC

Andrew Carnegie - *Scottish-American industrialist and philanthropist*

Harry Barclay – *Scottish farmer and businessman*

Iain Bruce – *Lawyer and doctor of homeopathy*

Michael Caine – *Film star*

Harry Carpenter – *Carpenter and serial entrepreneur*

Tom Cruise – *Film star*

Erna Dewachter – *Gardener, independent thinker*

Clint Eastwood – *Film star and movie director*

Lulu Goodman – *Flower girl and events organiser*

Jarvis Lawson – *Entrepreneur*

Zé Leal – *Chef and beach bum*

Cavaco Lobo – *Café owner and entrepreneur*

Sandy McKay – *Pub landlord and hotelier*

Mick and Mary – *Road haulier marketing consultants*

Henry Moore – *Artist and sculptor*

Chic Murray – *Scottish comedian*

Madame Murray – *Ballroom dance teacher*

My Grandfather – *Master Baker*

My Mum – *Scottish country dance teacher*

Noah – *Biblical character and investment portfolio consultant*

Rui Pinto – *Painter and restaurateur*

Pablo Picasso - *Painter, sculptor, print maker, ceramicist, stage designer, poet and playwright*

Jim Rankine – *Trawler skipper*

Iain 'Haggis' Reid – *Property consultant*

François Rodin – *Sculptor*

Oskar Schindler – *German industrialist*

Sikandar - *Restaurateur*

Mark Twain – *Author, humourist, entrepreneur, publisher and lecturer*

Max Wall – *Comedian and actor*

Other References

Aberdeen – *Scotland's third city*

Aberdeen Grammar School – *One of oldest schools in UK, founded 1257*

Borba – *Portuguese wine from the Alentejo region*

Dashing White Sergeant, Eightsome Reel, Strip The Willow – *Traditional Scottish country dances*

Disque Bleu – *French cigarette brand*

John Deere & Company – *Agricultural, construction and heavy machinery manufacturer*

Georgian era - *period in British history, 1714 to circa 1830–37*

Gitanes Bruin – *Full strength French cigarette*

Hill Samuel Financial Services – *Former retail distribution arm of leading* London *investment bank*

Klondike – *Region in Yukon, northwest Canada famous for gold rush of 1896-99*

Mercedes Benz – *Luxury marque motor car*

SelfPub Covers – *Online book publishers' resource*

RayBan – *Luxury brand spectacles*

Wake Up – *The author's leisure and learning breaks, personal mentoring and business guidance courses which he conducts in the sunny south of Portugal.* www.ibosocial.com/wakeup2wealth

You *can read all about Tom, his work and his latest publications at* www.tomriach.com

The Secret World Of Self-Employment

author have used their best efforts in preparing this book, they make no representations or warranties with respect to the accuracy or completeness of the contents of this book and specifically disclaim any implied warranties of merchantability or fitness for a particular purpose. It is sold on the understanding that the publisher is not engaged in rendering professional services and neither the publisher nor the author shall be liable for damages arising herefrom. If professional advice or other expert assistance is required, the services of a competent professional should be sought. This manuscript relates only the personal experience of the author.

This manuscript relates only the personal experience of the author. Where reference is made to equity options, crypto currency, stocks and shares and trading in these products, it is made only as a factual account of real experience. This book is not recommending that you do or do not use any specific trading system and readers considering participating in equity option or crypto currency trading are strongly advised to seek proper professional advice from an accredited stockbroker or investment advisor. The past performance of shares, equity options and crypto currencies are not necessarily indicative of future performance and the price of shares, equity options and crypto currencies can go in the opposite direction to that expected. No liability is accepted by the author or publisher or their servants or agents for the use by any readers of the information contained herein in any circumstance connected with actual trading or otherwise. The author is not a stockbroker nor investment adviser in terms of the Financial Services Act 1986 or otherwise and this book does not give any specific investment advice, it is not asking for investment funds, it is not inviting readers or offering to invite readers into any investment agreement directly or indirectly. The book is not advising readers on the merits of shares, equity options or crypto currencies nor is it advertising them and it is not inviting readers to buy or sell, or not to buy or sell, shares, equity options or crypto currencies. Whilst all reasonable care has been taken to ensure that the information contained in this publication is accurate and not misleading at the time of publication, neither the author, nor the publisher nor their servants nor agents, is responsible for any errors or omissions contained in this publication which is published for information only and does not constitute, or claim to constitute, investment advice.